ADVANCING
Word *for* Windows

Carol McKenzie • Pat Bryden

GW00504362

Heinemann

Heinemann Educational

a division of Heinemann Publishers (Oxford) Ltd,

Halley Court, Jordan Hill, Oxford OX2 8EJ

OXFORD LONDON EDINBURGH MADRID ATHENS BOLOGNA PARIS MELBOURNE SYDNEY AUCKLAND SINGAPORE TOKYO IBADAN NAIROBI HARARE GABORONE PORTSMOUTH NH (USA)

© Carol McKenzie and Patricia Bryden 1995

First Published 1995

95 96 97 98 11 10 9 8 7 6 5 4 3 2

A catalogue record for this book is available from the British Library on request.

ISBN 0 435 45420 X

Designed by Raynor Design using QuarkXPress™ 3.3 on the Apple Macintosh™

Printed in Great Britain by Thomson Litho, East Kilbride, Scotland

Screen shots reprinted with permission from Microsoft Corporation

Contents

Apostrophes
Spelling and grammar tools
 Errors of agreement
 Typographical and spelling errors
Advanced examinations: some points to remember
 Consistency of presentation
 Information to be located and inserted
 Documents with continuation sheet
 Abbreviations and unfamiliar words
 Indented text
Business letter on A4 letterhead
 Business letter layout: reminders
 Routeing of copies
 Printing on letterhead
 Inserting your name and other examination details
 Changing font size
 Letter with continuation sheet
 Page breaks in business letters
Page numbering (insert method)

Report or article
Character-style format
 Create a new style
 Apply a style
 Modify a style

Multi-page documents
 Method of working
 AutoCorrect
 Foreign accents

Footnotes
 Footnotes: Word's footnote command
 Footnotes: manual entry method
Ruled tables
 Ruled table: advanced features

About this book

Advancing Word for Windows has been written as a continuation text to *Introducing Word for Windows** and *Extending Word for Windows*** by the same authors. It has been designed as a progressive course and is suitable for use in the classroom, in an open-learning workshop or as a private study aid.

Advancing Word for Windows will help those preparing to take an advanced examination in word processing, using Word for Windows. However, the book would be equally useful to those who simply wish to extend their working knowledge of word processing using Word for Windows.

The syllabuses covered include:

RSA Word Processing Stage III Part 1

RSA Word Processing Stage III Part 2

Pitman Examinations Institute Advanced Word Processing

City & Guilds of London Institute Level 3

Students will derive most benefit from this book by working through the units in the order they appear. It has been designed to be a progressive course.

Previous experience

It is assumed that you have completed an intermediate (Stage II) word-processing course and are therefore familiar with conventional document layout and intermediate text-processing principles and practice. You should also be familiar with the hardware you are going to use (including the printer).

Format of the book

The book is divided into eight units, taking you through the word-processing functions you need to know for advanced examinations. Instructions for the preparation of particular documents are given at the beginning of each unit, followed by information on the Word for Windows commands relevant to the functions you will use. Exercises within each unit allow you to put the knowledge into practice.

Consolidation practice for each stage of learning is provided in Units 4 and 8.

Letterheads for use with the relevant exercises are provided for student use. These may be photocopied as necessary.

---

*   This publication covers the following syllabuses:
      RSA Computer Literacy and Information Technology (word-processing application)
      RSA Core Text Processing Skills (taken on a word processor)
      RSA Text Processing Stage I (Part 1)
      RSA Stage I Part 2 Word Processing
      Pitman Examinations Institute Elementary Word Processing
      City & Guilds of London Institute Level 1

**   This publication covers the following syllabuses:
      RSA Text Processing Stage II (Part 1)
      RSA Word Processing Stage II (Part 2)
      Pitman Examinations Institute Intermediate Word Processing
      City & Guilds of London Institute Level 2
      NVQ Administration Level 2 Units

Print-out checks for all exercises are given at the back of the book. These should be used for checking by both students and teachers/trainers.

Command boxes for Word for Windows functions are given when appropriate. Instruction is given on how to carry out the required function. The commands are given for keyboard, mouse and menu users. Students may select their preferred method.

The progress review checklist allows students to keep a record of progress through the exercises, noting any comments on topics if necessary. If completed at the end of each working session, the student can refer to this checklist to locate without delay the unit to be worked next.

The glossary of commands provides a comprehensive, alphabetically listed quick reference for all the Word for Windows commands introduced in the book. The commands are shown for keyboard, mouse and menu users.

How to use this book

If you are preparing for an examination, you are advised to work through the book unit by unit.

The book has been planned as a progressive course and some of the work you will do in the later units is based on text you will have keyed in earlier so *it is important to save your work.*

Working through a unit

1   When you see this symbol, read all the information before you begin. You may also need to refer to this information as you carry out the exercises.

2   When you see this symbol, carry out the exercises, following the numbered steps, e.g. **1.1, 1.2.**

3   Use your spelling tool to check your document. Proof-read your document carefully – the spelling tool does not find every error.

4   Use the print preview facility to check that your document is going to be correct when printed. If it is, save your work on to your floppy disk (usually in A drive). Then print your work.

5   Compare your document with the print-out checks at the back of the book. (If you are using this book in class, your tutor may also wish to check your work.) Correct any errors which you find in your work. Print the documents again if required to do so by your tutor. (If you are working on your own, you may not consider this necessary.)

6   Complete your progress review checklist. Then exit from Word for Windows or begin work on the next unit (as appropriate).

Do not delete files from your disk – you will need them later!

Introduction to Word for Windows

Microsoft Windows is a graphical user interface which allows the user to communicate with the computer. The graphical nature of the messages on screen makes Windows a user-friendly operating system. **Word for Windows** is a software package used for text processing which operates within the Windows environment.

When you start the *Word for Windows* program, the following **document window** will be displayed on screen:

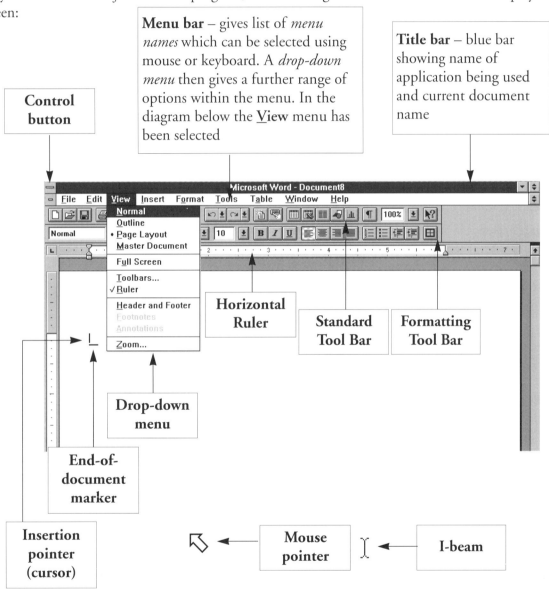

Menu bar – gives list of *menu names* which can be selected using mouse or keyboard. A *drop-down menu* then gives a further range of options within the menu. In the diagram below the <u>V</u>iew menu has been selected

Title bar – blue bar showing name of application being used and current document name

Control button

Horizontal Ruler

Standard Tool Bar

Formatting Tool Bar

Drop-down menu

End-of-document marker

Insertion pointer (cursor)

Mouse pointer

I-beam

When Word is carrying out a function, it may ask you to wait. The icon for this is the **hourglass** ⏳. Wait until the hourglass has disappeared from the screen before proceeding with the next step.

The **Status Bar** at the bottom of the screen displays information about the document on screen, e.g. the page number, section number, line number, column number, etc. For example:

| Page 3 | Sec 1 | 3/3 | At 1" | Ln 1 | Col 10 | 10:21 |

Menu

To select an option from the menu you can either:

- use the keyboard – press the underlined letter for the required menu option
- use the mouse – click the mouse pointer on the option required
- use a keyboard shortcut, e.g. **Ctrl + F** selects the <u>F</u>ind menu option (holding down the **Ctrl** key and then pressing the letter shown will activate the command)

A **tick** against a menu choice indicates that the option is currently in operation. When the tick is removed, the facility is 'switched off'. An **ellipsis** after a menu choice (e.g. <u>Z</u>oom...) indicates that you will be asked to give more information before the command can be executed.

Toolbars

To select an icon from the Standard or Formatting Tool Bar you:

Click: The mouse pointer ↖ on the icon

Each icon on the toolbars represents a different function. For example, clicking on the  print icon would activate the printer to print a copy of the current document. The use of icons is explained more fully throughout the book.

The function activated by each icon is shown in a **tool tip** which appears when the mouse pointer is positioned on the icon. (A fuller description appears at the same time in the **Status Bar** at the bottom of the screen.)

The **Bold** tool tip

When you click on an icon button it is 'highlighted' to show that the function is currently in operation.

Dialogue box

When Word needs to give or receive more information, a **dialogue box** is displayed on screen. You can move through the dialogue box using the **Tab** key or the **Arrow** keys on the keyboard, or you can use the mouse to move to the section you need. Word for Windows asks you to respond by presenting information, options or questions in different ways by using boxes and buttons (see page 5).

Spin box – click on the up and down arrows to change the display

Command buttons – click to carry out an action related to the dialogue box

Option buttons – click in circle to select. Black circle shows the option which is selected

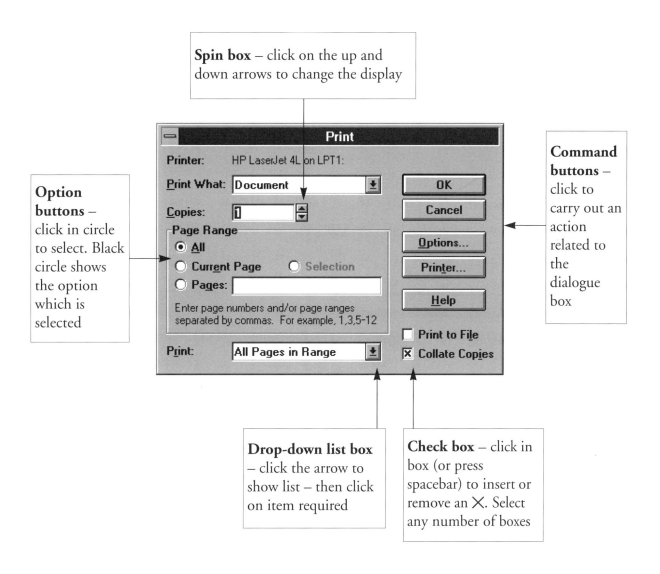

Drop-down list box – click the arrow to show list – then click on item required

Check box – click in box (or press spacebar) to insert or remove an X. Select any number of boxes

The Scroll Bars

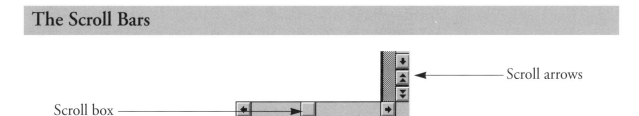

Scroll arrows

Scroll box

The **Scroll Bars** at the right side and bottom of the screen allow text to be scrolled by the use of the mouse, e.g. clicking on the ⊡ button will move the 'document frame' downwards so that the text moves up the screen.

Scroll Bar showing View buttons and left scroll button

The Scroll Bar also displays buttons to select the different ways in which a document can be viewed.

Using the mouse

The mouse is used to move a pointer to any required location on screen. The mouse has two buttons: **left** and **right**. As you move the mouse across the desk, an electronic sensor picks up the movement of the ball and moves the **mouse pointer** across the screen in the same direction.

* You use the mouse to *point* to the item you want on screen.

* You then *click* the mouse button (usually the left one) to highlight or *select* an option on screen (quickly pressing and releasing the button).

* Sometimes you *double-click* a mouse button (quickly pressing and releasing the button twice).

* You may also use a *dragging* action by holding down the mouse button, moving the mouse and then releasing the button.

The help menu

Word for Windows offers on-line **help** to users. The help command can be activated in two ways from the document screen:

* By selecting **Help** from the menu bar
* By clicking on the [▶?] icon on the Standard Tool Bar and then clicking on the feature on screen or keying in the name of the feature with which you require help

Selecting **Contents** from the help drop-down menu gives a list of the features available, e.g.:

Using Word
Step-by-step instructions to help you complete your tasks

Examples and Demos
Visual examples and demonstrations to help you learn Word

Selecting **Search for Help on…** from the help drop-down menu gives you the opportunity to key in the name of the feature with which you require help.

Selecting **Index** displays an alphabetical list of functions and features. You can move quickly through the list by clicking on the alphabetical button of the feature you require at the top of the index screen.

Selecting **Quick Preview** activates a learning program which introduces you to Word for Windows.

Selecting **Examples and Demos** allows you to access demonstrations of a range of Word features.

UNIT 1

Apostrophes, text-processing revision, business letter with continuation sheet

At the end of Unit 1 you will have learnt how to

- *use apostrophes correctly;*
- *identify and correct errors of agreement;*
- *identify and correct typographical and spelling errors;*
- *present material in a consistent style;*
- *produce a business letter in the fully blocked style;*
- *indicate enclosures and routeing on a letter;*
- *print a letter on A4 preprinted letterhead;*
- *change font size for a document; and*
- *produce a business letter with a continuation sheet.*

Note: The exercises in this book have been keyed in using the Arial font in point size 10. *Please use this font and point size for your work.*

 Apostrophes

In advanced examinations, you will be expected to know when to use an apostrophe and where it should be positioned in the word it relates to. An apostrophe is used to show that a letter (or letters) has been left out, e.g.:

don't	(*do not*)	haven't	(*have not*)
she'd	(*she had*)	you're	(*you are*)

1.1 Starting a new file, key in the following sentences using Arial point size 10, shortening the words underlined and putting the apostrophe in the correct place:

<u>You are</u> late! <u>We have</u> been waiting for you. Sit down and <u>we will</u> start or <u>there will</u> be no food left for you.

<u>Do not</u> say you <u>cannot</u> do the work. <u>It is</u> not difficult and <u>there is</u> no reason why you <u>should not</u> finish it.

(Leave this work on the screen. Do not save or print yet.)

More apostrophes

Apostrophes are also used to show possession – that something 'belongs' to someone or something, e.g.:

Nicola's pen	*(the pen of Nicola)*
The book's cover	*(the cover of the book)*
Tomorrow's paper	*(the paper of tomorrow)*
The day's work	*(the work of the day)*

If the word ends in 'ss', an apostrophe is added but there is no extra 's', e.g.:

The dress' zip	*(the zip of the dress)*

If there is more than one 'possessor', the apostrophe goes after the 's', e.g.:

The students' desks	*(the desks of the students)*
The girls' aunt	*(the aunt of the girls)*
The dresses' zips	*(the zips of the dresses)*

1.2 Key in the following sentences below the previous exercise, rearranging the underlined words and inserting the apostrophes in the correct places:

The glare of the sun caused the eyes of the player to lose sight of (the) ball of his opponent. The end of the game was announced and the victory of the winner was acknowledged by the captain of the other team.

The streets of the city were crowded as tourists and residents waited to see the car of the Mayor arrive at the entrance to the Club. The Freedom of the City was to be bestowed on the football team of the city and its manager.

(Leave this work on the screen. Do not save or print yet.)

Even more apostrophes

In speech, 'its' can mean two things: 'it is' (or 'it has') or 'belonging to it'. An apostrophe is used only when the full phrase of 'it is' (or 'it has') is shortened – the apostrophe shows that a letter has been missed out, e.g.:

It's good	*(It is good)*
It's said	*(It is said)*
It's up to you	*(It is up to you)*
It's been on my mind	*(It has been on my mind)*

But

The house has its door painted red.
We will improve its appearance.
The chair had its legs repaired.

1.3 Key in the following passage, below the previous exercises, inserting apostrophes where necessary:

Its your decision as to whether you wish to bring the dog on Saturday. Its well-behaved and the children like its friendly nature. They were pleased to hear that its recovered from its recent illness and they are looking forward to its coming so that it can play with its new toys and they can see for themselves that its fit and well again.

(Leave this work on the screen. Do not save or print yet.)

Apostrophes again

Apostrophes are sometimes used in the plural (when there is more than one) of words that are not usually used in the plural, e.g.:

> pro's and con's
> If's and but's
> 60's and 70's
> p's and q's

(*but*, more frequently, these words are shown without apostrophes).

1.4 Key in the following passage below the previous exercises, inserting apostrophes in the correct places:

We were always told to be careful to dot our is and cross our ts but the typewriter, which must date from the 1950s or 1960s, wouldnt print ws and ps and missed the tails off the ys, qs and gs!

1.5 Check your work on screen against the print-out checks at the back of the book. Correct any errors and print a copy of your work.

Spelling and grammar tools

Word for Windows' Spelling checker may help you to use apostrophes correctly, and you could use it as a final check. Word for Windows' grammar tool may help you to identify other errors, such as errors of agreement, but you should use this facility with caution as it may prompt you to make significant changes to an author's copy. This may not be acceptable to the author, and changes of that nature should *not* be used when working on examination papers – the copy must be followed exactly.

1.6 Use the spelling and grammar tools to check your work and then proof-read it yourself, comparing it with the print-out check at the back of the book. If you have made any errors, refer to the explanations on the use of apostrophes in the unit, and amend your text on screen. There is no need to save or print this work.

Errors of agreement

This type of error will appear in the manuscript text which you are copying, and in *retrieved text* in the examination. The errors will *not* always be indicated in advanced examinations – you are often expected to find these errors and correct them automatically as you key in the text.

As you are keying in text, you should make sure that what you are typing makes sense – 'listen' to what you are typing.

You should watch out for errors of agreement such as:

> This class of girls are irritating.

This should be keyed in as:

> This class of girls is irritating.

because there is only *one* class. If there were more than one class, you would key in:

> These classes of girls are irritating.

> The difference between the two word processing programs were demonstrated by the supervisor.

should be keyed in as:

> The difference between the two word processing programs was demonstrated by the supervisor.

because there are *two* programs but only *one* difference.

Typographical and spelling errors

The manuscript text which you copy will also contain some typographical and/or spelling errors. Remember always to use your program's spellcheck facility before you print your work!

Be careful of homophones, e.g.:

here	*and*	hear
their	*and*	there
course	*and*	coarse
hour	*and*	our

Spellcheck will not find this type of error – it's up to you to read the text and choose the correct version.

Advanced examinations: some points to remember

Consistency of presentation
Measurements, weights, times, money

You should always be consistent in the way you present information within a document. The following are examples of points you should watch out for.

Be consistent in the use of an abbreviation to represent a *measurement or weight*, such as **mm**, **cm**, **ft**, **in**, **kg**, **oz**, **lb**. For example, don't key in **30"** in one place and **24 in** somewhere else in the document. Be consistent – use either **"** or **in** but not a mixture of the two.

You may leave one space before the abbreviation, or no spaces, but you must be consistent. For example, don't key in **46kg** in one place and **46 kg** somewhere else in the document.

Stick to the 12-hour clock or the 24-hour clock when using *times*. For example, don't key in **1600 hrs** in one place and **7.30 am** somewhere else in the document. Be consistent in the use of **pm**, **o'clock**, **hrs**.

When using an abbreviation for *currency* (e.g. $, £, DM, F), stick to one method of presentation. For example, don't key in **£15** in one place and **£12.50** somewhere else in the document. Both amounts should show the pence (**£15.00** and **£12.50**). Don't key in **FF100** in one place and **100 French francs** somewhere else in the document. You should use either **£** or **p** but not both together in one amount – **£0.50p** is wrong.

Words and figures

Be consistent in the way you present *numbers* in a document. For example, don't key in **40 miles** in one place and **fifty-five miles** somewhere else in the document. Look through the text first and decide on words or figures. Think about these two examples:

- 1,234,650 is difficult to express in words.
- 1 looks strange as the first word of a sentence.

Other possible inconsistencies

Be consistent in using the *dash* (-) or the *hyphen* (-) between words and symbols. The keyboard symbol is the same, the spacing either side of the symbol is different. (A dash 'separates' words and has one space before and after. A hyphen 'joins' words and has no spaces before and after.) Don't key in **4 – 6** in one place and **16–21** somewhere else in the document. Also, don't key in **4 to 6** in one place and **16–21** somewhere else in the document. The word **to** can also be used in **3 to 4 weeks'** time, **Tuesday to Thursday**. Don't key in **Friday – Sunday** in one place and **Monday to Wednesday** somewhere else in the document.

Be consistent in the presentation of **per cent**. For example, don't key in **50%** in one place and **100 per cent** somewhere else in the document.

When keying in words which can be *spelt in two different ways*, make sure all occurrences match. For example, don't key in **organise** in one place and **organize** somewhere else in the document.

Be consistent in the amount of space you leave after *punctuation*. For example, don't leave **1 space** after a full stop in one place and **2 spaces** after a full stop somewhere else in the document.

You should standardize the *layout* of any document which you are producing. For example, don't mix paragraph styles (e.g. keep them all blocked to the left or all indented) and make all headings the same style (e.g. all in capitals or all in lower case and underlined).

Information to be located and inserted

There are two possible sources of information to be inserted into a task. It may be located either:

1 In another task in the examination paper; or

2 Through an announcement by the examination invigilator. (Early in an examination, the invigilator may read out a piece of information which is to be incorporated into any one of the tasks – *have a pencil handy so you can jot it down.*)

Documents with continuation sheet

You may be asked to prepare documents which will take up more than one sheet of A4 paper. This will require you to insert page breaks (new-page markers) in an appropriate place and to set automatic page numbering so that second and subsequent pages are numbered.

Abbreviations and unfamiliar words

In advanced examinations, you may find that words will be abbreviated without any indication that they should be expanded. Follow the rules you observed in intermediate examinations. Copy all foreign and unfamiliar words carefully to avoid errors.

Indented text

A section of text (typescript or manuscript) may be indented for emphasis in any of the tasks in advanced examinations. You should retain the indentation even though no specific instruction is given to do so.

 Business letter on A4 letterhead

Business letter layout: reminders

You should have already learnt how to set out a business letter as part of your earlier text-processing training. A business letter is written on behalf of an organization and is printed or typed on the organization's own letterhead, which gives all relevant details such as address, telephone and fax numbers.

In advanced examinations, you may be asked to produce a business letter on a preprinted letterhead. Use the following format:

- Block everything at the left-hand margin – indent paragraphs or centre items if shown in copy.
- Date the letter with today's date – use automatic date-insertion facility to save time.
- Use open punctuation – no punctuation except in the body of the letter.
- Leave at least one clear line space between the different parts of the letter, and between paragraphs.
- If the salutation is formal, e.g. 'Dear Sir or Madam', finish your letter with the complimentary close 'Yours faithfully'.
- If the salutation is informal, e.g. 'Dear Mrs Smith', finish your letter with the complimentary close 'Yours sincerely'.
- Leave several clear lines for the person sending the letter to write his or her signature.

- Special marks such as CONFIDENTIAL, PRIVATE, PERSONAL, URGENT, FOR THE ATTENTION OF, etc., should be given some form of emphasis such as bold, underlining or capitalization. (The special mark should also be inserted on the envelope.)
- The enclosure mark is usually placed at the end of a letter with one clear line space above and below it.

Routeing of copies

It is normal practice for the sender to keep one copy of a letter or memo for reference. Additional copies may be required for other people and this is indicated at the foot of the document.

Instructions may be given as follows:

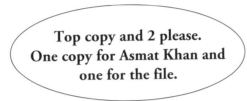

Top copy and 2 please.
One copy for Asmat Khan and
one for the file.

The routeing indication is inserted at the bottom of the document (under any enclosure indication), e.g.:

Copy: Asmat Khan

      File

When all the copies of the document have been printed, it is normal practice to indicate the destination of each copy by ticking (or underlining in coloured pen or using a highlighting pen).

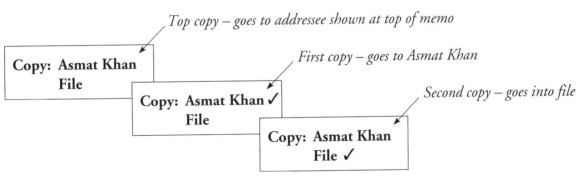

Printing on letterhead

In Word for Windows the top margin is usually set by default to 1 inch. When printing on a letterhead, the top margin *on the first page only* should be increased to accommodate the printed heading. (Second and subsequent pages are printed on plain paper.)

You may need to measure the depth of the letterheaded paper you intend to use, and to experiment to find the top margin measurement required. Find out how to insert letterheaded paper into the paper feed tray of your printer so that the document is printed in the correct position.

Change the top margin for letterheaded paper:

Mouse and menu

Key in the whole document before carrying out this procedure

Position the pointer immediately before the first letter of the document

Select: **Format, Paragraph**

Key in: **Required measurement** in **Spacing, Before** box (you may use any unit of measurement – e.g. 1 inch or 2 cm or 25 mm). Click on **OK**

Remember, Word's default top margin is 1 inch. To leave a 2 inch top margin, key in 1" in the Before box. This will add 1 inch to the existing default margin of 1 inch.

Note: The above setting will be changed to a point-size measurement and will remain selected until it is changed or deleted.

Inserting your name and other examination details

It is normal practice in an examination to key in your name, centre number and the task number as Line 1 of a document. However, when printing on a letterhead, these details are best positioned flush with the right margin on the same line as the date, e.g.:

1 January 1995   Your name Centre No 88888 Document 1

(In Word for Windows, type the date at the left margin, set a right-aligned tab stop at the right margin, press the tab key to move to this tab stop and then key in your name, etc.)

Changing font size

The letter may be a long one and you may decide to use a continuation sheet. However, if the letter will almost fit on one sheet, you may decide to reduce the font size slightly. Before printing, use print preview to check that all of the letter is present.

(*To change font size for a whole document:* Select: Whole document by pressing **Ctrl + A**, then select a lower number in the font-size box on the Formatting Tool Bar.)

Exercise 1A

1.7 Starting a new file, key in the following letter, using Arial font size 10. Print one copy. Use filename **EX1A**.

Letter to Mrs L Porter, The Coach House, Station Rd, Oxenwood, KEIGHLEY, West Yorkshire, BD22 4CH.   Ragged R Margin.
Please mark urgent and use a NMTA letterhead.

Dr Mrs P_   (Heading: ROADSAFE PLAN)

You have recently made enquiries about the our new (R_ Plan) CAPS wh is currantly presently being offered to long-standing, valued customers such as yourself. I enclose a leaflet giving full details, together w an application from.

✓ The insurance scheme plan gives additional cover to that which you already rec under our existing scheme and as a member of our org, (you are already) there wl be no need for you to take an medical examination. You wl automaticlly be accepted on to the R_ P_ provided you live in England, Wales, Scotland, the Isle of Man or the Chanel Islands).

As well as been covered for accidents in yr own vehicle, you will also be covered whilst traveling in someone elses' car as a passenger. The plan extends to world-wide pedestrian and passenger/public transport travel for the insured. ←

It is an unfortunate fact that if you are unfortunate enough whilst travelling to be injured, you may be of work for some time. You may even be unable to continue in yr former occupation but the bills will still have to be payed.

Motor-cyclists' are covered under our 'wings' scheme.

Please consider the attached leaflet over the next seven days. Simply select the type of cover you require, complete the application form & return it to us in the envelope provided. You will rec yr policy within 4 days + you may then read and study it thoroughley before committing yourself. We look foreward to hearing from you in the near future.
Yrs sincly   NATIONAL MOTOR AND TRAVEL ASSOCIATION

A B AXLEFORD
Customer Services Officer

Exercise 1B

1.8 Starting a new file, key in the following letter using Arial font size 12. Before saving and printing, reduce the point size to 10 so that the letter will fit on one sheet. Use filename **EX1B**.

Letter to Hermann & Free Ltd, 210-216 Larches Rd, Whiteacre Pk, LEEDS, LS26 3FX. Use a justified right margin and a PORTALS letterhead.

Our ref 95/10/GDENQ   Mark for the attention of Mr B N Free

Dr Sirs

embolden and underline please

PORTALS GARAGE DOORS

Further to yr telephone enquiry of (yesterday's date), I have pleasure in ~~forwarding~~ sending you ~~a copy of~~ copies of our colour brochures illustrating our full product range. An up-to-date trade price list is also enclosed.

Doors are ~~made~~ manufactured in timber, steel or GRP (moulded fibreglass) in a wide variety of finishes. A choice of door operation is provided: canopy, non-protruding & tracked.

Full performance tests is carried out after installation + materials are tested for durability. Consistency is ensured by manufacturing methods supported by BS5750 standards.

We feel that the selection of garage doors to suite the house style and local enviroment are an important factor in providing a ~~super~~ ~~quality~~ home and we are sure you wl find a style wh wl enhance yr new development at Rose Dell. Please contact me if you require further information. The usual trade terms' and conditions apply.

The security aspect is not overlooked. We realize that many house holders use these garages for the storage of valued and valueable items such as bicycles and gardening equipment, and we have paid ~~particular~~ special attention to locking systems. All of our doors are supplied w a high security system as standard. Remote controle operation is increasingly popular and is available as part of our range.

run on

As you requested, I am sending a copy of this letter and copies of brochures to your Sheffield Office for the attention of Mr S Driver. I hope that he will be impressed by the service we can provide. // I look forward to furthering our bus association.

Yrs sncly

MR S DRIVER

N GATESBY
Sales Manager

Letter with continuation sheet

The letter may be too long to fit on one sheet even if the font size is reduced. (It is not a good idea to reduce font sizes too much as the text can become difficult to read.) When a letter takes up more than one page, the first page should be printed on letterheaded paper and the second page should be printed on plain paper. You will have to decide where to insert a hard page break to form Page 2 and this page should be numbered. (You do not normally number the first page.)

Remember, in an examination, your name and exercise number should be displayed on both pages.

Page breaks in business letters

Page breaks should be inserted in sensible places within a document so that it is easy to read. Word will show a 'soft' page break (a horizontal dotted line) on screen when the maximum number of lines has been used. The printer will start a new page at this point.

A 'hard' page break is inserted by the operator and is displayed as a horizontal dotted line with the words 'page break' in the centre of the line. You should get into the habit of inserting hard page breaks after all other text formatting and amendments have been carried out and just before printing.

Consider the following points when paginating (inserting page breaks into) a document:

- The complimentary close of a letter (Yours…) should never be the *only* text on the last page. Ideally, there should be at least three or four lines of text above the complimentary close.

- You should not divide a word between one page and the next.

- You should not leave only the first line of a paragraph at the bottom of a page (a 'widow'). You should not carry forward only the last line of a paragraph on to the next page (an 'orphan').

Insert a new-page break

When keying in a long document, Word automatically inserts 'soft' page breaks for you. You can insert a 'hard' page break whenever you want to start a new page – e.g. the start of a new chapter.

Keyboard	Mouse and menu
Position insertion pointer where you want to insert the page break:	
Press: **Ctrl + ↵ (return)**	Select: **Insert, Break, Page Break, OK**

Widow/orphan control

Word allows you automatically to avoid widows and orphans. Check that your program is defaulted to the following option:

Mouse and menu
Select: **Format, Paragraph, Text Flow**

Check that the widow/orphan box is displayed as follows:

> **Pagination**
> ☒ **Widow/Orphan Control**

(All other boxes should be blank.)

Page numbering (insert method)

The second and subsequent pages of a multi-page document should be numbered. Word allows you to set the page numbering once – consecutive page numbers will then appear automatically on all pages (except the first one) starting with a number **2** on the second page.

Keyboard	Mouse and menu
Move pointer to required position	Select: **Insert, Page Numbers**
Press: **Alt + Shift + P**	
(page number appears on screen)	

The **Page Numbers** dialogue box is displayed on screen:

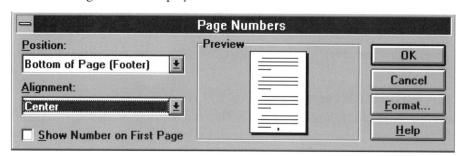

- Page numbering offers a choice of **Position, Alignment, Show Number on First Page**.
- The **Preview** box shows the page number in position.

Select from the page numbers dialogue box as appropriate:

Button	Action
Position	Select position on page *vertically* – bottom or top
Alignment	Select position on page *horizontally* – left, right, centre (inside and outside are used with binding margins)
Show Number on First	Remove ✗ to omit number on first page (this will also remove any header or footer text)
Preview	Displays page number in position chosen
Format	Allows format of page number to be selected, i.e. Arabic, roman, letters

Note: Page numbers show on screen in page layout view and print preview only.

Exercise 1C

1.9 Retrieve the file EX1B and add the following text just before the paragraph which begins 'Please contact me…'

> You may be intersted to no that our new showroom wl be opened on (next Sat's date) at the Highfields Bus Pk. (in Unit 10) The opening ceremony will take place at 12 noon & wl be followed by ~~food &~~ refreshments. I have pleasure in enclosing eight VIP invitation vouchers for (members of your firm) the use of). A CAPS (prize draw) is planned & the winner will rec a weekend brake for 2 at the 'Leisuretime' hotel of there choice. Additional prizes will include meals at the Lotus Garden restaurant and tickets for ~~shows~~ performances at Yorks' Grand Theater. I hope that you can attend our showroom opening and look forward to meeting you.

1.10 Set page numbering, suppressing this feature on Page 1.

1.11 Insert a hard page break in a sensible place.

1.12 Save and print a copy of your work. Use filename **EX1C**.

UNIT 2

Applying and modifying styles

At the end of Unit 2 you will have learnt how to

- *create, apply and modify character styles to text.*

You will also have practised and revised all the text-editing techniques you have previously learnt in the production of a report or article.

i Report or article

An advanced word-processing examination usually includes a report or article which may take up one or two pages. The task is to be keyed in by you and may test any (or all) of the items from the following list of word-processing functions:

- ragged/justified right margin
- change of line spacing within a document
- insetting/indenting of text
- changing of line length
- moving blocks of text
- errors of agreement
- typographical errors
- apostrophes
- abbreviations
- manuscript correction signs.

Refer to the glossary if you need to refresh your memory on the instructions for any of these word-processing functions and conventions, and refer to Unit 1 for previous notes on consistency of presentation for measurements, weights, times, money, words and figures. (A list of commonly abbreviated words was given in Unit 1 of *Extending Word for Windows*.)

Points to remember

1   It is easier to set a header to show your name, centre number and task number when a document takes up more than one page.

2   Multi-page documents should usually have pages numbered – but not always the first page.

3   You should insert page breaks in sensible places.

4   Follow the usual procedures for making sure that your work is completely accurate – proof-read very carefully, spellcheck and preview before printing.

Exercise 2A   **2.1**   Starting a new file, key in the following document as shown, *without any text emphasis or formatting*. Save as **EX2A**.

(NTMA) — in full please

Double line spacing and unjustified margin
ARIAL 10

ROADSAFE PLAN   5 clear lines

Apply Now!

Don't leave it to late. Apply to join our new Roadsafe Plan today! Complete the Application Form within the next 7 days and take advantage of our special introductry offer. Your policy will be with you within 4 days and you then have fourteen days in which to study the plan before you finally committ yourself. Post your application in the pre-payed envelope.

Introductory Offer

As soon as we receive the payment of your first premium, we will sent you a ~~stylish~~ attractive Clock ✓ Radio with our compliments. If you decide to adopt the new Roadsafe Plan within 7 days of receiving your policy, you will also receive a beautiful writing set containing a classic black onyx NMTA fountain pen and ball-point pen. These valuable items would cost at least £30 in the high street shops.

The Benefits

If you have an accident whilst travelling and you are off work for at least 10 consecutive working days, you will rec £90.00 per week for up to 2 years. [If you were fatally injured whilst travelling, your estate would rec a substantial cash payment of £100,000.

Indent by 1" (25 mm) at left

[Adults aged under 25 and over 65 rec 60 per cent of the benefits; children 25%]

At each renewal date, the premium increases automatically by 5 per cent but we guarantee that you wl not be asked to pay a higher premium however many claims you make.

Extra Cover

Not only will you and your family be covered for accidents in yr own vehicle, you will also be covered as a passenger in someone elses' car. Shd you be injured by a motor vehicle as a pedestrian, you are also covered. Any fare-paying public transport, anywhere in the world, is included in the plan.

LUMP SUM PAYMENTS ← Initial caps please

A lump sum of £120,000 is payable if you permanently lose the use of two limbs or the site in both eyes. £60,000 is payable for the loss of the use of 1 limb or the sight in 1 eye.

Daily and weekly Payments

You may be paid £90 per day if you have to spend time in hospital as an in-patient. The maximum ~~number of days~~ time for this payment is 365 consecutive days. You may be paid £110 per week if you are unable to continue with your ~~usual~~ normal ~~job~~ occupation for at least two weeks.

Guaranteed Cover

If you are eligible (over the age of ___ and a NMTA member), your acceptance onto the Roadsafe Plan is garanteed. Just complete the form & post it today!

CAPS

This benefit is payable for a minimum of 3 weeks & a maximum of eighteen months.

Age for eligibility
= over 21

Character-style format

Reports and articles often include a main heading and several subheadings. It is important that the headings are presented in a consistent format, for example in the same font and font size, and with the same emphasis (bold, underline or italics). Word's Style facility allows you to determine a format for headings (and other text if necessary) to ensure consistency. You may find this useful in examinations as well as in day-to-day work.

Create a new style

Word's Style function allows you to group together a set of formatting instructions (using the font dialogue box) and to save these instructions under a given name. For example, you may wish your main headings to be in Times New Roman, size 14, bold, centred and underlined. To save time, all these formatting commands can be grouped and saved together. They can then be applied to text in one action.

Key in your text, without formatting, and then create styles to be applied to selected portions of the text.

Mouse and menu

Select: **F**ormat, **S**tyle

The **Style** dialogue box is displayed on screen

- Click: **N**ew in the **Style** dialogue box
- Key in a name for the style in the **N**ame box, e.g. **Mainhead**
- Select: **Character** from the **Style T**ype drop-down menu
- Click: The **F**ormat ↓ button
- Select: **F**ont from the drop-down menu

The **Font** dialogue box is displayed on screen:

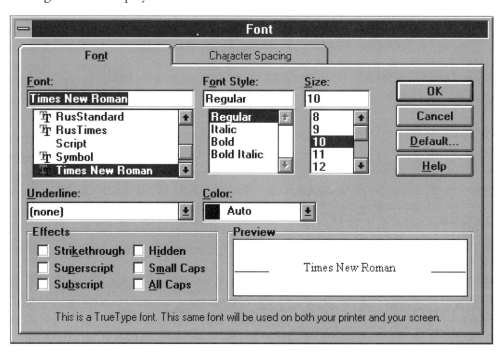

The dialogue box shows the formatting commands currently in use.

- Select: The text format you require from the different drop-down menus available (e.g. Font, Font Style, Size, etc.). The **Preview** box shows how the text will look in your document.

Click: **OK** to confirm your selection

Click: The **Add to Template** box at the bottom of the dialogue box (this allows you to use the style in all new documents as well as in the current one)

Click: **OK** in the **New Style** dialogue box

Click on: **Close** on the **Style** dialogue box (the style is stored in the style drop-down menu on the Formatting Tool Bar, ready for use)

Apply a style
Mouse and menu

Select: The text which is to be formatted to a certain style

Select: The style name from the style drop-down menu on the Formatting Tool Bar *or*

Select: **Format, Style** and select style required

Click: The **Apply** button

Repeat the above steps as necessary throughout the document.

2.2 Following the instructions for creating a style, create and name two styles for headings as follows:

STYLE NAME	FONT	FONT SIZE	FORMAT
Mainhead	Arial	14	Bold, underline
Subhead	Arial	12	Bold

2.3 Retrieve the document EX2A if it is not already on screen. Apply the style you created and saved as **Mainhead** to the first two lines of the document.

2.4 Apply the style you created and saved as **Subhead** to all other headings in the document.

2.5 Use the spelling and grammar tools to check your work and proof-read it yourself carefully.

2.6 Save and print your document, using the same filename **EX2A**. Check your print-out with that at the back of the book. If you find any errors, correct them and print again if necessary.

Exercise 2B **2.7** Starting a new file, key in the following document as shown, *without any text emphasis or formatting*. Save as **EX2B**.

LEISURE TIME HOTELS ⏜(ARIAL 10 please) (Double spacing except where shown. Justified margins.)

*

Countryside and Countrywide Weekend Breaks

single spacing

Whether you want to unwind in the piece of the countryside, live it up in the capital or visit places of interest, Leisuretime Hotels can offer you the perfect solution. With over 200 hotels, there's sure to be one wh is ~~perfect~~ just right for you.

We offer the widest choice of locations and the best prices wherever you ~~want to go~~ and whatever *you* ~~want to do.~~ Our Two and three-day breaks are available all year round.

* (Please leave at least 1" or 2.5 cm where * is shown)

Your Hotel

You can be sure of a warm welcome and great service. All rooms have a private bathroom and you will be served a full English breakfast every morning. Tea and Coffee making facilities are available in all rooms. Colour TV is provided in all hotel rooms.

Your Family

(✓) Children sharing a room with *parents* ~~adults~~ in a 3 or 4-bedded room stay FREE. Under 5 yrs of age, children may eat FREE. If you are taking a weekend break for 3 nights, two children under 15 may have a FREE room! Full details of other special FREE offers are *shown on* ~~available~~ Page 10 of the current brochure. (Babysitting services are usually available if booked in advance.)

Midweek Breaks

If you can manage to get away during the week, you can miss the crowds and the traffic jams! You may stay for two or more consecutive nights between Mon and Thursday for only ~~£35.00~~ per person *pernight*. Dinner, bed & breakfast is included in the price.

(Please change line length to 5" or 13cm for whole document)

Weekend/Breaks *Budget* at selected hotels

Stay for two or more nights and choose from bed and breakfast, or dinner, bed and breakfast. Prices start from only £30 per person per night.

If you can manage to get away for only 1 night, perhaps after visiting an exhibition or attending a function, we will be pleased to accomodate you. *Special* One-night breaks are available on Fridays or Saturdays only. The price is the same - £30 p— p— p— n—.

TOURING BREAKS ← (Initial caps only)   (travel by car ♯)

Our unique voucher system means that you can stay for one or two nights at one hotel and then drive to another hotel for the third (and forth) night. Accom is at certain ~~selected~~ participating hotels ~~and~~ which offer the same high standards of service as all of our hotels. ←

single spacing [
Plan your route and tell us where you'd like to stay. We'll pre-book your hotels for you and save you the worry. You'll know that a warm welcome and a 3-course dinner will be waiting for you at the end of a hard days' sightseeing!
] *Indent ½" (1.25 cm) at both sides*

(The maximum stay in any hotel is 2 nights)

Coach & Rail Breaks

single spacing [
Let someone else worry about the driving. Relax and admire the countryside as you travel to your chosen hotel. Our Booking *staff* Service/ wll be able to advice you on the best route and the quickest method of travel.
]

*

(Midweek Break = £50 pppn)

Booking Service

single spacing [
You can ring us for the cost of a local call at any time. The Service operates 24 hrs a day. Our advisers will help you to make the best selection at the best price.
]

Ring us on 01425-861-610 today.

Modify a style

In Word for Windows, you can modify a style which you created previously and save it under the same style name.

Mouse and menu

Select: **F̲ormat, S̲tyle**

Click: The **M̲odify** button

Key in the name of the style you wish to modify in the **N̲ame** box

Select: **F̲ont** from the **F̲ormat** drop-down menu and make the appropriate changes (the **Preview** box shows how the text will look in your document)

Click: **OK** to confirm your modifications

Click:The **A̲dd to Template** box if you want to use the modified style in all new documents as well as in the current one

Click: **OK** in the **Modify Style** dialogue box

Click: **Close** in the **Style** dialogue box

2.8   Modify the styles you created earlier as follows:

STYLE NAME	FONT	FONT SIZE	FORMAT
Mainhead	Footlight Mt Light	16	Bold
Subhead	Footlight MT Light	14	Underline

Note: If the Footlight MT Light font is not available to you, use a font of your choice.

2.9   Retrieve the document EX2B if it is not already on screen and apply the style you modified and saved as **Mainhead** to the first line of the document.

2.10 Apply the style you modified and saved as **Subhead** to all other headings in the document.

2.11 Save and print your document, using the same filename **EX2B**. Check your print-out with that at the back of the book. If you find any errors, correct them and print again if necessary.

UNIT 3
Multi-page document, AutoCorrect, foreign accents

At the end of Unit 3 you will have learnt how to

- *complete a multi-page document using advanced features;*
- *enter a text footer with automatic page numbering;*
- *use Word's AutoCorrect command; and*
- *apply foreign accents to the text.*

i Multi-page documents

In an advanced examination, a 'header and footer' task may extend to four pages. Refer to the glossary if you need to refresh your memory on setting headers, footers and document pagination. You may be required to carry out any or all of the text-editing techniques you have previously learnt, but the instructions will be more complex and varied. Read through the task before you attempt any reformatting procedures. Ensure you understand all the instructions and amendment signs, and that you don't miss any.

Method of working for multi-page documents

The following is a method of working that has proved successful and one which you might like to adopt. Using this method means that you will return to the top of the document and work through it several times, carrying out a different function each time. This might seem time-consuming but if you always use the method you will get into a routine and you will be sure that you have not missed anything out. There is an added advantage in going through a document several times – you might spot an error that can be corrected as you scan through the work! Make sure you know how to move the cursor around your document as quickly as possible.

1. Set the *header(s)* as requested in the draft. Check if you need to put on *page numbering*, starting from Page 2, as well as any specified text *footer*. Use the preview facility to check that any header, footer or page number is correctly positioned.

2. Carry out all the necessary *text amendments*, e.g. inserting or deleting of text. Also check carefully for abbreviations, spellings, errors of agreement, grammatical errors, consistency of presentation, typing errors, punctuation errors, etc. You should check any text you are asked to retrieve as well as the text you key in.

3. *Move* and/or *copy* blocks of text as requested throughout the whole document.

4. *Find* and *replace* text as requested.

5. *Allocate space* and *indent* or *inset margins* as requested.

6. *Paginate* your document sensibly, or as requested (read the instructions).

7. *Spellcheck* the whole document.

8. *Proof-read* the whole document, comparing it word for word with the copy.

9. Use Word's *print preview* facility to make sure your document is going to be printed correctly.

10. Finally, *print* your work.

AutoCorrect

You can customize the AutoCorrect facility to correct misspellings, expand abbreviations, automatically insert words which are difficult to spell, or automatically enter text or graphics which you use repeatedly.

By adding a word you often type incorrectly to the AutoCorrect list, the next time you key it in incorrectly, as soon as you leave a space or a punctuation mark, Word will automatically correct it for you. For example, you may often key in **adn** instead of **and**.

If you frequently use a word which is difficult to spell, such as a medical term or a complicated name, you can add the word to the AutoCorrect list. For example, you could use **Tric** as a representative shortform for the word **Trichlorethylene** or **Zol** to represent the surname **Zoledziejewski**.

Select: <u>A</u>utoCorrect from the <u>T</u>ools menu

The **AutoCorrect** dialogue box appears on screen:

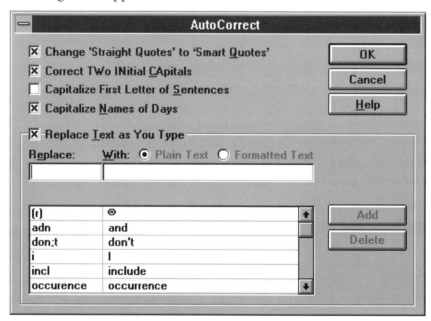

In the **Replace** box: Type in the word as you would normally mistype it, or the abbreviation, or the representative shortform. The entry can be up to 31 characters but cannot include spaces

In the **With** box: Type in the correct text as you want it to appear in the document

Click: The **Add** button

Click: **OK**

Foreign accents

You can apply foreign accents to text by pressing a combination of keys on the standard keyboard. For example, when keying in the words *table d'hôte*, to produce *ô* first press: **Ctrl + ^** and then press: **o**

To insert a foreign accent with an upper-case letter, press the key combination then press shift + the letter. For example, to enter the name *ANDRÉ*, first press: **Ctrl + '** and then press: **Shift + E**

àèìòù	ÀÈÌÒÙ	Ctrl + ` (accent grave), the letter	å Å	Ctrl + @, *a* or *A*
áéíóúý	ÁÉÍÓÚÝ	Ctrl + ' (apostrophe), the letter	æ œ Æ Œ	Ctrl + &, *a, o, A, O*
âêîôû	ÂÊÎÔÛ	Ctrl + ^ (caret), the letter	ç Ç	Ctrl + , (comma), *c* or *C*
ãñõ	ÃÑÕ	Ctrl + ~ (tilde), the letter	ð Ð	Ctrl + ' (apostrophe), *d* or *D*
äëïöüÿ	ÄËÏÖÜŸ	Ctrl + : (colon), the letter	ø Ø	Ctrl + /, *o* or *O*

Practice exercise

3.1 Starting a new file, instruct Word's AutoCorrect facility to use the representative shortform **Sp** for the word **Sphygmomanometer**. Then, key in the following passage:

USE OF THE SPHYGMOMANOMETER

Place the bag of the Sphygmomanometer over the brachial artery and bind it in position by its band. Then inflate the Sphygmomanometer bag while applying a stethoscope over the artery just above the bend of the elbow. A muffled sound will be heard which stops when the level of the systolic pressure is reached. Note the level of the mercury. Check by inflating the Sphygmomanometer bag about 10 mm more, then slowly release the valve. Note the level of the mercury when the first tapping sound is heard. The average of the two figures is the systolic pressure.

Continue to deflate the Sphygmomanometer bag. The sounds become muffled and then finally disappear. The level of the mercury at this point is the diastolic pressure.

Remove the Sphygmomanometer band.

3.2 Close the file without saving ready for the next exercise – you do not need to print this exercise.

Exercise 3A

3.3 Retrieve the file you saved earlier as EX2A. Look carefully at Exercise 3A – you are asked to make a number of amendments to the document including move, copy, delete, change line spacing, margin justification, search and replace, header, footer and page numbering. You may also be able to use the AutoCorrect facility you have just practised.

Work your way through the document, following the method of working described at the beginning of this unit.

Save and print your document using filename **EX3A**. Check your print-out with that at the back of the book. If you find any errors, correct them on screen, save your document again and print again if necessary.

NATIONAL MOTOR AND TRAVEL ASSOCIATION

[centre + remove underline]

ROADSAFE PLAN

[Change Roadsafe Plan to Roadwise Plan throughout the document]

Apply Now!

Don't leave it too late. Apply to join our new Roadsafe Plan ~~today~~ *asap*! Complete the Application Form within the next ~~7~~ *14* days and take advantage of our special introductory offer. Your policy *[-this offer is available for a limited period only]* will be ~~with~~ *sent to* you within 4 days and you then have ~~14~~ *21* days in which to study the plan before you finally commit yourself. ~~Post your application in the pre-paid envelope.~~ Ⓐ

Introductory Offer

[inset this section by 2" (50 mm) at the right margin to allow room for a photo]

As soon as we receive the payment of your first premium, we will ~~send~~ *forward* you a stylish Clock Radio with our compliments. If you decide to adopt the new Roadsafe Plan within ~~7~~ *14* days of receiving your policy, you will also receive a beautiful writing set containing a classic ~~black~~ *silver-plated* ~~onyx~~ NMTA fountain pen and ball-point pen. These valuable items would *normally* cost at least £30 in the high street shops.

(leave the rest of this page blank)

The Benefits

[enter the header: NMTA PLAN at top right of every page and remove page numbering from page 1]

If you have an accident whilst travelling and you are off work for at least 10 consecutive working days, you *will* receive £90 per week for up to 2 years.

If you were fatally injured whilst travelling, your estate would receive a ~~substantial~~ cash payment of £100,000.

[remove indent + put in single line spacing with a line length of 4" (100 mm)]

Adults aged under 25 and over 65 receive 60% of the benefits; children 25%.

At each renewal date, the premium increases automatically by 5% but we guarantee that you will not be asked to pay a higher premium however many claims you make.

Extra Cover ← *(amend __all__ the subheadings as follows: remove bold and change to capitals)*

Not only will you and your family be covered for accidents in your own vehicle, you will also be covered ~~as a~~ *if you are a* passenger in someone else's car, ~~Should you be injured by a motor vehicle~~ *or if you are involved in an accident* as a pedestrian, ~~you are also covered.~~ Any fare-paying public transport, anywhere in he world, is included in the plan, *including:*

a) taxis + buses
b) trains
c) ships
d) ferry boats
e) hovercraft
f) aeroplanes

Ⓑ

~~**Lump Sum Payments**~~

iii) A lump sum of £120,000 is payable if you permanently lose the use of 2 limbs or the sight in both eyes. £60,000 is payable for the loss of the use of 1 limb or the sight in 1 eye.

Daily, ~~and~~ Weekly /Payments *and Lump Sum*

Whether you are involved in an accident or lose yr job, the bills wl still keep comming in!

i) You may be paid £40 per day if you have to spend time in hospital as an in-patient. The maximum time for this payment is 365 consecutive days.

ii) You may be paid £110 per week if you are unable to continue with your normal occupation for at least 2 weeks. This benefit is payable for a minimum of 3 weeks and a maximum of 18 months.

(move to top of page 2)

please put all enumerated items in single line spacing but with one clear line between items. Also, indent enumerated sections by ½" (13mm) at left margin.

Guaranteed Cover

If you are eligible (over the age of 21 and a NMTA member) your acceptance onto the Roadsafe Plan is guaranteed. *You won't have to take a medical or even answer questions about yr health.*

JUST COMPLETE THE FORM AND POST IT ~~TODAY!~~ *asap* *(remove capitalisation and copy to Ⓐ)*

Use a justified margin throughout the document.

insert at Ⓑ:
Accidents on a motor bike are excluded but motor cyclists can be covered with the NMTA Wheels Scheme

Exercise 3B

3.4   Retrieve the file you saved earlier as EX2B. Edit and amend the document as requested, following all the instructions carefully.

Save and print your document using filename **EX3B**. Check your printout with that at the back of the book. If you find any errors, correct them on screen, save your document again and print again if necessary.

LEISURETIME HOTELS ← centre + underline

Change to a RAGGED right margin and use single line spacing throughout the document.

Countryside and Countrywide Weekend Breaks

Whether you want to unwind in the peace of the countryside, live it up in the capital or <u>visit places of interest, Leisuretime Hotels can offer you the perfect solution.</u> With over 200 hotels, there's sure to be one which is just right for you.

NP Choose from the bright lites + sights of a big city, the architecture, traditional character + heritage of an historic town, the forrested fells and mountain peaks of the Lakes + Highlands, or the rolling countryside of a charming country village.

Your Hotel

except where indicated

You can be sure of a warm welcome and great service. All rooms have a private bathroom and you will be served a full *traditional* English breakfast every morning.

Tea and coffee making facilities are available in all rooms. Colour TV is provided in all hotel rooms. On half-board breaks, three-course table d'hôte dinner w coffee or yr choice of 3 courses from each hotels' own "Spécialité Menu".

Your Family

B

c) Children sharing a room with adults in a 3 or 4-bedded room stay FREE. d) Under 5 years of age, children may eat FREE. e) On a 3-night ~~If you are taking a~~ weekend break ~~for 3 nights,~~ 2 children under 15 may have a FREE room! ~~(Babysitting services are usually available if booked in advance.)~~ Full details of *many more* ~~other~~ special FREE offers are shown on Page ~~10~~ *12* of the current brochure.

please start all enumerated items on a new line and indent by ½" (13mm) at left margin, ie: a) ____   b) ____

Midweek Breaks

If you can manage to get away during the week, you can miss the traffic jams and the crowds! You may stay for 2 or more consecutive nights between Monday and Thursday for only *forty-five* ~~£50~~ per person per night. Dinner, bed and breakfast are included in the price.

Move the Midweek Breaks section to C

1

Weekend Budget Breaks

(remove underline and add bold to all subheadings)

Stay for 2 or more nights and choose from bed and breakfast, or dinner, bed and breakfast. Prices start from only £30 per person per night.

If you can manage to get away for only 1 night, perhaps after visiting an exhibition or attending a function, we will be pleased to accommodate you. Special 1-night breaks are available on Fridays or Saturdays only. The price is ~~the same~~ £30 per person per night.

©

Touring Breaks

(Start this section on a new page)

Our unique voucher system means that you can travel by car and stay for 1 or 2 nights at one hotel and then drive to another hotel for the third (and fourth) night. Accommodation is at certain participating hotels which offer the same high standards of service as all of our hotels. The maximum stay in any hotel is 2 nights.

Plan your route and tell us where you'd like to stay. We'll pre-book your hotels for you and save you the worry. You'll know that a warm welcome and a 3-course dinner will be waiting for you at the end of a hard day's sightseeing!

Coach and Rail Breaks

(and scenery)

Let someone else worry about the driving. Relax and admire the countryside as you travel to your chosen hotel. Our Booking Service staff will be able to advise you on the best route and the ~~quickest~~ *most appropriate* method of travel.

(leave at least another 2" (50mm) here)

(indent this section by 1" (25mm) at left and right margins)

Booking Service

NP

You can ring us for the cost of a local call at any time. The Service operates 24 hours a day. Our advisers will help you to make the best selection at the best price. Ring us on 01425-861-610 today.

(Copy to end of first paragraph on page 1)

* enter a header: JOYWAYS
  at top right of each page
* enter a footer: REF: JB/Flyer
  at bottom left of each page
* retain page numbering on all
  pages, starting from page 6

delete the space at (A)
and insert this text

Get Away with leisuretime

You can feel confident when you book yr leisuretime brake. Their are no hidden extra's. Part of our great value package is our "Privilege Voucher Pack" – a book of discount vouchers giving you special discounts on admission to exciting local attractions.

insert
at
(B)

Family fun begins when every child is given a FREE leisuretime Fun Pack to keep them amused whilst you unpack. leisuretime Hotels have a grate deal to offer cost-concious families, w many saving money offers also available during school holidays:

a) Most Hotels offer a FREE baby-listening service.

b) Cots, highchairs & FREE baby food are available on request.

Change leisuretime to JoyWays throughout the document

4 Consolidation 1

Task 1

Key in this letter, using a justified right margin, to: Mr & Mrs FT Sandal, West Lodge, St Clement's Ave, Trimmlington, ROCHLEY, RY12 1AG. Mark the letter PERSONAL please. Save as TASK1 and print a copy on a Distant Lands letterhead.

Dear Mr & Mrs S___

Holiday Opp of a Lifetime! DISTANT LANDS [Heading in CAPS & bold]

As a valued customer of our sister co, 'Holiday Dreams', I wd like to ~~give~~ offer you the privelege of /viewing our /pre new holiday brochure for the coming season before it's release to ~~agents and~~ the general public. [D__ L___ holidays, as suggested by the name, covers destinations world-wide while maintaining the same high standards & competative prices as 'H__D__'. We can transport you to the Caribbean ~~in the~~ (west) or to Thailand in the Far East, w many other destinations in between ~~such as~~ including ✓ Africa, India and Egypt.

Our special introductory offer to you is available until (give date for last day of month after next). All you have to do is ~~to book a~~ select the holiday of your choice from the enclosed broachure. When you have confirm yr booking thro yr travel agent, you wl save up to £100 per person on a 14-night holiday. *// As you wl see from the D__ L__ brochure enclosed, we offer superb deals for families w ~~discounts~~ reductions from 10% ~~to 50%~~ for all 2-11 yr olds ~~to~~ and 50 percent for the first child. Infants of 0 to 2 yrs can travel for only £75 pounds. (They wl not be serve ~~food~~ a and are expected to sit on ~~their~~ parents knee during the flight) Group reductions are available for ~~18~~ 15 or more full-fair paying passangers, and self-catering accom ~~presents~~ offers savings for the third and 4th adult sharing a room.

[margin note: Indent ½" at L & R]

For the 'young at heart', a romantic wedding honeymoon or 'second honeymoon' in a perfect situation setting can be ~~incorporated into yr holiday~~ arranged for destinations in the Carribean, and Goa on (Sri Lanka) Indias west coast. Leave all the details to our wedding staff – they wl make all the necy arrangements including the marriage license, and a beautiful setting for yr special day. ↑ (will ensure)

The honeymoon service begin w a bottle of champagne on yr outward flight and ends w a candle lit diner, at yr holiday hotel (on the last evening).

Our 'Romance in D_L_' video can be ~~bought~~ purchased for £7.99p – see how yr dream could come true!

A copy of this letter has been ~~forwarded~~ sent to your travel agent, Rochley Travel, & I hope that you wl visit them at yr earliest opp to book yr holiday of a life time and take advantage of our superb savings.

Yrs sincerley
DISTANT LANDS PLC

Alison Louis

(More 1st and 2nd paras on this page – 'For the 'young at --- holiday hotel' to the point marked * after the indented para. (Keep as separate paras and do not indent)

(Please put D_L_ in bold, except in video name)

Task 2

Please use a ragged right margin and change indented paras to blocked style. Single line spacing except for first and last paras. Save as TASK 2 and print a copy.

Choosing yr perfect holiday is part of the pleasure of the whole exp. However, you shd choose w care to ensure full enjoyment.   *(double spacing)*

GENERAL GUIDELINES ← *(spaced caps & centre)*
(3 clear lines after heading)

<u>Making an informed choice</u>

for example,

Read the details in the brochure carefully. The info will be accurate but, you cannot afford to miss the fact that a hotels' access to the beech is by steep steps if you have infants or disabled persons in your party. Ask your agent for further details of your choice before booking.

(VISAS) AND (PASSPORTS) ← *Make all side headings like this – CAPS no underline*

s   *Allow*
British visitors passport are not valid for all destinations. ~~Give~~ yourself sufficient time to obtain a full passport. Some countries also require a visa. Check with your travel agnet and embassies. If your passport is not a British one, you must ensure that you can ~~re-enter~~ into the UK.
gain re-entry   *(relevant)*

<u>Health</u>
Consider the temperture charts in yr ~~holiday~~ brochure – you probably want to feel comfortable, not too hot or too cold. Be aware of standards of hygiene (differing) and the ~~possibility~~ ✓ ~~prevalence~~ of diseases if yr party includes children & older people. Yr local health center can advice on recommended (inoculations, vaccinations) and other precautions.

<u>Further Assistance</u>   These are general guidelines only. Your t_ a_ wl be able to give detailed info & help. Read the small print in the holiday brochure to – you may not be aware of all the implications ~~if~~ unless you ~~dont~~ do.   *(double spacing)*

NB Max length of pregnancy = 28 wks

make last paragraph pleae

Types of accomodation

The choices is endless: ~~from Youth Hostels through pensions and house boats to 5-star hotels~~. *

in choosing accom

Cost is probably the most important factor/but consider the amount of work which may be (enormously) involved in self-catering. Eating out varies/in price between resorts and countries - ~~find out,~~ obtain a rough idea before you make your final decision. (On any holiday, there may be extra for costs/which you had not planned ~~for~~ - such as use of use of sunbeds, sports facilities, local travel, extra films for your camera, etc.

* Campsites
Youth Hostels
Bed & Breakfast
Guest Houses & Pensions
Small & Large Hotels
Houseboats & Yachts

Put this list below heading at * and inset 1" (25mm) from left

FLIGHTS

The flight time may varie between 2 hrs and 14 hrs. Long distance flights ~~may~~ sometimes include a re-fuelling stop. Some airlines ~~will not allow~~ are reluctant to allow women who are more than ___ weeks pregnant to fly without a dr's letter. Check w yr agent _and_ yr dr. /When packing, remember that there is a maximum (allowance ~~for~~ baggage), & only 1 small piece of handluggage is ~~permitted~~. ✓
allowed

Task 3

Retrieve Task 2 and amend as shown. Double spacing except where shown otherwise. Number pages at bottom R starting at P3. Use a header INDIAN HOLIDAYS

~~GENERAL~~ GUIDELINES FOR INDIA

Shorten line length to 4" or 10cm for this para

single spacing

Choosing your perfect holiday is part of the pleasure of the whole experience. However, you should choose with care to ensure full enjoyment.

MAKING AN INFORMED CHOICE

emphasise all side headings

Read the details in the brochure carefully. The information will be accurate but, for example, you cannot afford to miss the fact that a hotel's access to the beach is by steep steps if you have infants or disabled persons in your party. Ask your agent for further details of your choice before booking.

*

leave at least 3" here (7.5cm)

Use justified margins please throughout

PASSPORTS AND VISAS

~~British visitors passports are not valid for all destinations.~~ Allow yourself sufficient time to obtain a full passport, *and* ~~Some countries also require~~ a visa. Check with your travel agent and ~~relevant embassies~~ *the High Commission of India*. If your passport is not a British one, you must ensure that you can gain re-entry into the UK.

leave at least 1" (25cm) here

HEALTH

Consider the temperature charts in your brochure - you probably want to feel comfortable, not too hot or too cold. Be aware of differing standards of hygiene and the prevalence of disease if your party includes children and older people. ~~Your local health centre can advise on recommended vaccinations, inoculations and other precautions.~~ // A coarse of anti-malaria pills are recommended, & you shd be inoculated ~~for~~ against Cholera.

It is generally a good idea to by bottled minral water. Dont forget to take w you any ~~special~~ *specific* ✓ medicines you are likely to need.

Move to top of page 6

TYPES OF ACCOMMODATION (PAGE 4)

The choice is endless:

1 Campsites
3 Youth Hostels
2 Bed and Breakfast
4 Guest Houses and Pensions
5 Houseboats and Yachts
6 Small and large Hotels

Retain single spacing for numbered items. Retain 1" indent.

Cost is probably the most important factor in choosing accommodation. ~~but consider the amount of work which may be involved in self-catering. Eating out varies enormously in price between resorts and countries~~ Obtain a rough idea before you make your final decision.

On any holiday, there may be extra costs for which you had not planned - such as use of sun beds, sports facilities, local travel, extra films for your camera, etc. *Copy to ✱*

FLIGHTS

The flight time may vary between ~~2~~ 8 hours and 14 hours, and ~~Long-distance flights~~ sometimes include a re-fuelling stop. Some airlines are reluctant to allow women who are more than 28 weeks pregnant to fly without a doctor's letter. Check with your agent <u>and</u> your doctor.

When packing, remember that there is a maximum baggage allowance, and only one small piece of hand luggage is permitted.

Start 3rd page here (Page 5)

CURRENCY MONEY

You wl have to complete a Declaration Form on arrival to state the amount of cash, notes and travellers' checks you have bought. There is no limit to the amount. It is very important that you change ~~currency~~ money only thro' authorised money changers. No Indian currency (rupees) may be imported or exported.

When in India ---

Footware shd not be worn in Muslim, Hindu, (Sikh or Jain) temples. It is best not to give money to beggars, and you shd be careful not to succumb to 'bargains' from street vendors – use only government emporia and shops on the list published by the Dept. of Tourism.

You shd cover yr head before going into a Sikh shrine.

Please change 'holiday' to 'Indian holiday' throughout the document

Make this para the last one of the document – on Pg 6

FURTHER ASSISTANCE

Single spacing
These are general guidelines only. Your travel agent will be able to give detailed information and help. Read the small print in the holiday brochure too - you may not be aware of all the implications unless you do.

UNIT 5 *Footnotes and ruled tables*

At the end of Unit 5 you will have learnt how to

- *enter footnotes using superscripted numbers;*
- *enter footnotes using Word's automatic footnote command;*
- *rearrange table items in a specified order;*
- *enter horizontal and/or vertical column headings;*
- *adapt a table to fit on the specified paper size;*
- *modify the layout and work out tab settings for an advanced table display; and*
- *produce a table with ruled lines.*

i Footnotes

Footnotes (and endnotes) are used to explain in more depth, or provide references for, a particular point made within the body of the document text. A footnote comprises two linked parts: a footnote symbol, such as a * or a superscripted character (e.g. [1]), which is placed as a reference mark in the body of the text next to the word, figure or phrase which needs further explanation, and the same symbol repeated later in the document with the explanatory text. A superscripted character is printed slightly above the standard line, e.g. 8.5^2

Example

The special discount price for bulk orders[1]
applies during the winter quarter[2] only.

[1] Quantities of ten or more
[2] November–February

There is *no space before* the footnote reference mark in the body of the text. There is at least *one space between* the footnote character and explanatory text.

You can enter footnotes manually, using keyboard symbols or superscripted characters. Or you can use Word's automatic footnote command which automatically numbers footnote marks or allows you to create your own custom marks. With this latter method, Word will automatically renumber the footnote reference marks if you add, delete or move any of them.

Footnotes: Word's footnote command

To enter a footnote reference mark

Position the insertion pointer immediately after the last character of the word, figure or phrase requiring a footnote.

Select: **Footnote** from the **Insert** menu *or*

Press: **Alt + Ctrl + F**

The **Footnote and Endnote** dialogue box appears on screen:

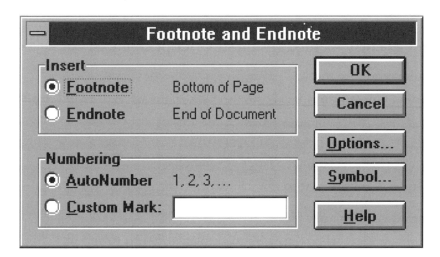

Click: **Footnote** button (unless it is already selected)

Click: **AutoNumber** button automatically to number the footnote

To modify the footnote:

Click: **Options, All Footnotes:**

Place At: Lets you choose whether to place the footnote explanatory text immediately 'Beneath the text' or at the 'Bottom of the Page'

Number Format: Lets you select a different footnote display, e.g. **a,b,c**, or **i,ii,iii**

Start At: Lets you specify the character to start numbering from

Numbering: Lets you specify print notes at different locations in the document

Click: **OK**

To customize the footnote as a symbol:

Click: **Symbol**

Click: On a symbol from the choice displayed

Click: **OK**

Click: **OK**

To enter the footnote explanatory text

As soon as you exit the Footnote and Endnote dialogue box, Word automatically prompts you to enter the explanatory text at the bottom of the page (or other specified location in the document). Remember to leave at least one clear space before the note text. Click in the main document to leave the explanatory text.

To view footnotes

Double-click the footnote reference mark. In normal view, the footnotes appear in the note pane; in page layout view, the footnotes appear at the location they will be printed in the document.

To move or delete a footnote

Operate normal **cut** and **paste** commands.

To format a footnote

Operate normal text-formatting commands, e.g. bold, italic, font size, etc.

Footnotes: manual entry method (using superscript characters or keyboard symbols)

To enter a footnote reference mark

Position the insertion pointer immediately after the last character of the word, figure or phrase requiring a footnote:

Press: **Ctrl + Shift + =** to change the font to **superscript**

Key in: The footnote character (number, letter or symbol)

Press: **Ctrl + Shift + =** again to revert to normal text

To enter the footnote explanatory text

Position the insertion pointer where you wish the explanatory text to appear – this is usually at the end of the page or at the end of the document:

Key in: The same footnote character that was used as a reference mark – this does *not* need to be in superscript. Leave at least one clear space, then key in the explanatory text

---

Exercise 5A

5.1 Key in the following document using Word's automatic footnote command to enter the footnotes (the footnotes will be displayed at the bottom of the page unless you select the 'Place at' option and choose 'Beneath text').

<u>SHERDALE HALL</u>

This month sees Sherdale in a vibrant, colourful and cosmopolitan mood. The cultural capital of the North is an apt description - for where else would you find Irish Music, Chinese costumes and French boules.

On Saturday, there are two events with an international flavour: Sherdale Hall is to host a French Summer Fete[1] at "1300 heures" - that's one o'clock. This will be followed in the evening by an Irish Festival Night[2] at eight o'clock with music from Folk, Country and Irish groups plus a team of Irish dancers.

---

[1] The fete will take place outside, weather permitting, otherwise in the Main Hall.
[2] The Irish night will take place in the Mozart ballroom.

5.2 Position the insertion pointer immediately after the last word in the first paragraph, **boules**. Insert another footnote, using the **Options** facility to

- select: **Beneath Text** from the **Place At** drop-down menu of location options
- select: **a, b, c,** from the **Number Format** drop-down menu of display options

Enter the explanatory text for the footnote as: **A game of French *bowls*.**

Note how Word automatically renumbers the footnotes you entered previously in the correct sequence. You will have to use page layout view or print preview to see the footnote explanatory text displayed beneath the main passage of text.

5.3 Save and print your document using filename **EX5A**. Check that your print-out appears as shown below, paying particular attention to the footnotes. If you find any errors, correct them, save your document again and print again if necessary.

SHERDALE HALL

This month sees Sherdale in a vibrant, colourful and cosmopolitan mood. The cultural capital of the North is an apt description - for where else would you find Irish Music, Chinese costumes and French boules[a].

On Saturday, there are two events with an international flavour: Sherdale Hall is to host a French Summer Fete[b] at "1300 heures" - that's one o'clock. This will be followed in the evening by an Irish Festival Night[c] at eight o'clock with music from Folk, Country and Irish groups plus a team of Irish dancers.

[a] A game of French *bowls*.
[b] The fete will be held outside, weather permitting, otherwise in the Main Hall.
[c] The Irish night will take place in the Mozart ballroom.

 # Ruled tables

Data is often presented in columns within letters, memos and reports to convey information quickly and clearly. Tabulated columns of information are also used for separate tables and accounts. As an alternative to normal tabulation procedures, Word for Windows has an automatic Table Wizard facility which you can use quickly to produce table layouts with ruled borders. (Details of tabulation procedures were provided in the second book of this series.)

Ruled table: advanced features
Making the table fit on the page

If the table is quite large, you may also need to give consideration to making it fit on the page/paper size being used. If you think the table won't fit using normal settings, you could

- reduce the left and right margins to $\frac{1}{2}$ inch – this is the least amount acceptable
- wrap the text around on to the next line in the column
- reduce the font size.

Rearranging the table items

To rearrange or sort the table into a particular order, you could

- use a piece of scrap paper to note down, in advance, the order in which the entries should be keyed in
- key in the entries as displayed, then use cut and paste functions to rearrange the items in the required order
- key in the entries as displayed, then use Word's Sort command to sort the items in the required order.

(Full instructions on the Sort command were provided in the second book of this series.)

Vertical column heading

A vertical heading takes up one character per line and is read downwards instead of across. The number of characters in the heading will determine the depth of the vertical-column heading area. Depending on the method you are using to complete the table, either

	P
	A
	G
ITEM DESCRIPTION	E
Walnut Grandfather Clock	5
Brass Carriage Clock	8

- 'shrink' the column, using the mouse to drag the column dividing line until it is the appropriate width (if you are using Word's automatic table facility) *or*

- set a tab stop in the normal way to position the vertical heading (if you are using tabulation procedures).

Creating ruled tables using Word's table facilities and Table Wizard

Ruled lines

When you you use Word's automatic table command, the table layout appears on screen surrounded by a grid of dotted lines. Word does not print out the dotted gridlines that divide the table cells. To print the vertical and horizontal lines of the table, you must instruct Word to apply borders to the table. If you wish to make the document look more professional, you can also apply shading to some of the table cells, e.g. the column headings.

There are several different ways to apply borders (ruled lines). You can predetermine the borders and shading of the table layout using the Table command or Table Wizard. Or you can apply borders and shading after you have created the main table display using the Borders and Shading command from the Format menu, or by using the Borders Tool Bar. Depending on the layout you wish to create, you may even use a combination of methods.

To remove ruled lines from part of a table, i.e. a single cell, see 'Borders Tool Bar' section below.

Borders and shading method

Position insertion point where you want the table to be placed:

Click: ▦ table button on the Standard Tool Bar (a drop-down grid of rows and column cells appears on screen)

Select: The number of rows and columns required by dragging the mouse pointer across the grid until the bottom of the grid displays the correct layout (e.g. 3 × 4 Table). The grid will increase in size as you drag the mouse. Release the mouse button

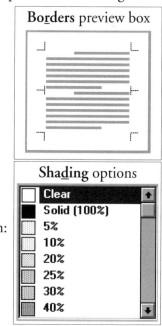

Select: **B**orders and **S**hading from the **F**ormat menu:

- Select: **B**orders

- Select: A line style from the list of **St**y**le** options

- Select: **N**one, B**ox** or **G**rid from the **Presets** options

- Modify the layout if necessary by selecting any of the lines in the **Bo**r**ders** preview box

- Click: **OK**

To apply shading: *First* select: The cells in the table you want to shade, then:

Select: **B**orders and **S**hading from the **F**ormat menu:

- Select: **S**hading

- Click: The **Sha**d**ing** percentage you want from the list of options

- Click: **OK**

Table menu method and Table Wizard

Position insertion pointer where you want the table to be placed:

Select: <u>T</u>able, <u>I</u>nsert Table

The **Insert Table** dialogue box appears on screen:

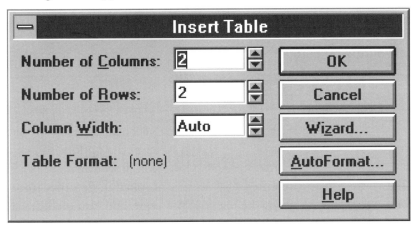

Select from the table dialogue options as appropriate:

1	**Number of <u>C</u>olumns**	Enter the required number of vertical columns
	Number of <u>R</u>ows	Enter the required number of horizontal rows
	Column <u>W</u>idth	Accept the default setting (auto) or select a column width
		Click: **OK**

optional:

2	**<u>A</u>utoFormat...**	The **AutoFormat Table** dialogue box appears on screen:

Select: The design you want from list of options in the **Forma<u>t</u>s** box – for a basic style of ruled table, choose **Grid 1** (to remove all formats, select: **none**)

Click: **OK**

Formats to Apply and **Apply Special Formats To** allows you to select different effects for different parts of the table

The **Preview** box allows you to see the table as it will appear with the chosen format

Choose from the special formatting options given – the different effects available can be seen in the Preview box

Click: **OK** when you have made all your choices.

3	**Wizard**	A 'Wizard' prompts you to select from given options so that Word can automatically set out your document in the way you require. The Table Wizard is often used to create tables quickly.

The **Table Wizard** dialogue box appears on screen.

Word prompts you to choose an appropriate style for the table layout:

Click: The appropriate button for the **Style** required

Select: <u>N</u>ext> to move to the next set of options

Continue to answer the questions in the Wizard as they appear

Select: <u>F</u>inish when your layout is complete

Borders Tool Bar

The Borders Tool Bar is used to apply borders and/or shading to a table, or parts of a table, *after* it has been created.

To apply borders and/or shading to the whole table

Position insertion point in table:

Select: **Select Table** from the **Table** menu *or* press: **Alt + 5** (on numeric keypad)

Click: ⊞ **Borders** button on Formatting Tool Bar

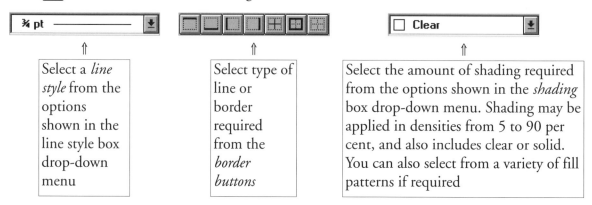

Select a *line style* from the options shown in the line style box drop-down menu	Select type of line or border required from the *border buttons*	Select the amount of shading required from the options shown in the *shading* box drop-down menu. Shading may be applied in densities from 5 to 90 per cent, and also includes clear or solid. You can also select from a variety of fill patterns if required

To apply borders and/or shading to specific cells of a table (e.g. the heading rows)

First, select: The cell(s) you wish to apply a border and/or shading to

Select: The appropriate option(s) from the Borders Tool Bar

To remove borders/lines from part of a table (e.g. the top/bottom of a single cell)

First, select: The cell(s) you wish to remove lines from

Select: **None** from the **Line Style** drop-down menu box

Click: On the appropriate **Border** button on the **Borders Tool Bar** (i.e. top border, bottom border)

Note: If the line you wish to remove *divides two cells*, you will need to remove it from *both cells*.

Setting tabs inside a table

You can set tabs inside a table just as you would normally. This is useful if you need to set a decimal tab or if you are working with subdivisions.

- *To set a tab for one cell only:* Set the appropriate tab-stop type on the horizontal ruler using normal tabulation procedures.

- *To set a tab for a section of the table:* First, select: The data, then set: The appropriate tab-stop type on the horizontal ruler.

- *To set a tab for a whole column:* Position the insertion pointer in the column you want the tab stop to affect:

  Select: **Select Column** from the **Table** menu, then set: The appropriate tab-stop type on the horizontal ruler.

Press: **Ctrl + Tab** to move to tab stops in a table (if you press the tab key on its own, you simply move to the next cell).

Remember: Whenever you set a tab stop you immediately cancel out any default tab stops set to the *left* of it. Default tabs to the *right* are unaffected.

Moving around in a table

Arrow keys	You can move around the table using the appropriate arrow keys
Tab	Moves right one cell (or inserts a new row when pressed in the last table cell)
Shift + Tab	Moves left one cell
Ctrl + Tab	Moves to next tab stop in the cell
Alt + Home	Moves to first cell in same row
Alt + End	Moves to last cell in same row
Alt + PgUp	Moves to top cell in column
Alt + PgDn	Moves to bottom cell in column

Or Click: The mouse pointer in any cell you want to move to.

Changing column width in a table

Mouse	**Menu**
Select: The column(s) to be changed	Select: The column(s) to be changed
Point to the column dividing line and press the left mouse button down (the pointer changes to a ↔ double-headed arrow)	Select: **Table, Cell Height and Width, Column**
Drag the column dividing line to the left or right to increase or decrease the column width as appropriate	Enter: The appropriate measurement in the **Width of Column** box
Release the mouse button	Click: **OK**
	(*Note:* You can also specify the amount of space between columns if required.)

Changing row height in a table

Mouse	**Menu**
Select: The row(s) to be changed	Select: The row(s) to be changed
In page layout view ▤ point to row marker dividing line on vertical ruler:	Select: **Table, Cell Height and Width, Row**

Row marker (dividing line)

The pointer changes to a vertical double-headed arrow ↕

Enter: The appropriate measurement in the **Height of Rows** and **At** boxes

Click: **OK**

(*Note:* You can also specify any row alignment and/or indent if required.)

Drag the row dividing line up or down to increase or decrease the row height as appropriate

Release the mouse button

Inserting columns and rows in a table

Position the insertion pointer at the place you wish to make the insertion:

Select: **Table, Select Row** *or* **Select Column**

Select: **Table, Insert Rows/Insert Columns**

Or press: The right mouse button and select: **Insert Rows/Insert Columns**

Or with the insertion point in the table, click: **Table button** on Standard Tool Bar (a row is inserted above the position of the insertion pointer)

Deleting columns and rows in a table

Position the insertion point at the place you wish to make the deletion:

Select: **Table, Select Row** *or* **Select Column**

Select: **Table, Delete Rows/Delete Columns** *or*

Select: **Table, Delete Cells, Delete Entire Column** *or* **Delete Entire Row**

Or press: The right mouse button and select: **Delete Rows**

Or select column to be deleted. Press: The right mouse button and select: **Delete Columns**

Joining/merging cells in a table

Select: The cells to be joined together. Select: **Table, Merge Cells**

Splitting cells in a table

Select: The cells to be split. Select: **Table, Split Cells**

Subdivided and multi-line column headings

If the copy you are working from shows subdivided or multi-line column headings, remember to include these in your tab settings. Remember, even if you are using Word's Table facilities you can set tabs using normal tabulation procedures within the table layout.

A *multi-line column heading* means that the column heading appears on more than one line:

COURSE	START DATE	END DATE	COST £
(col 1)	(col 2)	(col 3)	(col 4)

A *subdivided column heading* means that the column heading may be divided into two or more subheadings:

COURSE	COURSE DATES		COST £
	START	END	
(col 1)	(col 2 + 3)		(col 4)

If you are using Word's automatic table facility, your table layout would appear as:

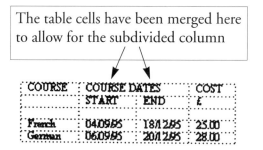

The table cells have been merged here to allow for the subdivided column

COURSE	COURSE DATES		COST £
	START	END	
French	04.09.95	18.12.95	25.00
German	06.09.95	20.12.95	28.00

Practice exercise

5.4   Apply the instructions given in this unit to create the following:

- A 6 × 6 table using Word's **Insert Table** command from the **Table** menu, applying the **Table Autoformat** facility to apply different borders and shading.

- A 6 × 6 table using Word's **Table Wizard** feature to apply different borders and shading.

- A 6 × 6 table using the **Insert Table** button on the **Standard Tool Bar** and applying different borders and shading through the **Borders and Shading** command from the **Format** menu.

- A 6 × 6 table using the **Insert Table** button on the **Standard Tool Bar** and applying different borders and shading through the **Borders Tool Bar**.

- A 6 × 6 table and, following the example below, 'shrink' one of the columns in a table for a vertical heading and practise laying out subdivided and multi-line column headings:

COLOUR	WEIGHT	SIZE	PRICE OF ITEM (£)		P A G E
			PURCHASE	SELL	

Tip: Enter the 'E' of PAGE in a separate cell

- Use the **Borders Tool Bar** buttons to remove the appropriate lines in the heading rows so that the layout of your ruled table appears as below. You will first need to select the cell(s) you wish to remove lines from then, select: **None** from the **Line Style** drop-down menu box. Click: The **Top Border** or **Bottom Border** button on the **Borders Tool Bar**. Remember, the dotted line separating some of the cells will not be visible when the table is is printed:

COLOUR	WEIGHT	SIZE	PRICE OF ITEM (£)		P A G E
			PURCHASE	SELL	

Tip: Remember to remove the line from both cells

- Use the **Borders Tool Bar** buttons to apply 10 per cent shading to the heading rows so that the layout of your ruled table appears as below. Remember, you will first need to select the cells to be shaded. Print out your table and check that it looks like the example given below. You do not need to save the file – this exercise is just for practice.

COLOUR	WEIGHT	SIZE	PRICE OF ITEM (£)		P A G E
			PURCHASE	SELL	

Exercise 5B

5.5 Starting a new file, enter the table as shown below. Save and print your document using filename **EX5B**. Check your print-out with the exercise shown below. If you find any errors, correct them on screen, save your document again and print again if necessary.

MICROWAVE COOKING

VEGETABLE	COOK[1]	PROPORTIONS		M I N S	SERVING SUGGESTIONS
		SIZE	WEIGHT		
Cauliflower	T or S	Florets	n/a	4	Cheese sauce
Spinach	WT	Leaves	n/a	1	Melted butter
Artichokes	T or S	Pieces	25 g (1 oz)	4	Melted butter or white sauce
Courgettes	S	Whole[2]	50 g (2 oz)	3	Melted butter
Artichokes	T	Small	200 g (8 oz)	8	Butter & lemon juice
Cabbage	S	Shredded	n/a	4	Melted butter

---

[1] S = Separator, T = Trivet, WT = Without Trivet
[2] If using 1-inch slices, increase cooking time to 4 minutes.

5.6 Rearrange the items by **VEGETABLE** name so that they appear in ascending order. Save and print your document using the same filename **EX5B**. Check your print-out with that at the back of the book. If you find any errors, correct them on screen, save your document again and print again if necessary.

Exercise 5C

5.7 Starting a new file, enter the table as shown below.
Rearrange the items so that they appear in ascending order of **PAGE** number. Save and print your document using filename **EX5C**. Check your print-out with that at the back of the book. If you find any errors, correct them on screen, save your document again and print again if necessary.

REF NO	ITEM DESCRIPTION	P A G E	SIZE	COST PER ITEM[1]	
				UNDER 10	OVER 10
43Z	Harvest Sweatshirt	9	34-36	£16.99	£14.99
18BR	Layton Sweatshirt[2]	5	36-38	£17.99	£15.99
49D	Mayling Sweatshirt	6	34-36	£16.99	£14.99
26C	Fenn Sweatshirt	4	40-42	£18.99	£16.99

1 Orders of over 50 qualify for a further discount.

2 Limited stocks available on this item.

Move the PAGE column so it appears between REF NO and ITEM DESCRIPTION

Exercise 5D

5.8   Starting a new file, enter the table shown below.
Save and print your document using filename **EX5D**. Check your print-out with that at the back of the book. If you find any errors, correct them on screen, save your document again and print again if necessary.

DESKTOP PCs ← (centre underline)

MACHINE	PRICE £	SPECIFICATION DETAILS			HARD DISK	m S D²
		PROCESSOR	SPEED	MEMORY[1]		
A) DIGIT-EX SYSTEMS ← (bold)						
Digit-ex Magna	2774.00	Pentium	66mHz	16-192Mb	520 Mb	7
Digit-ex Classic	825.00	i486 SX	33MHz	4-64Mb	210 mb	5
Digit-ex Royale	1459.00	i486 DX	33MHz	4-128mb	250Mb	6
B) JRM DESKPRO SYSTEMS ← (bold)						
ZX3 Plus	1300.00	i486 DX	33MHz	4-64 Mb	250 mb	5
ZX4 Super	1845	Pentium	66MHz	8-64 Mb	270mb	5
Value-line ZX2	899.00	i486sx	33 MHz	4-32Mb	200mb	3
C) COMPUSTYLE TECHNO SYSTEMS ← (bold)						
CTS basic	599.00	Cx486SLC	33 MHz	2-16mb	100mb	4
CTS de-luxe	1885.00	i486 DX2	33MHz	8-64Mb	340Mb	5
CTS exec	1569	Am486 DX	40MHz	4-64Mb	620mb	4

[1] Standard & ~~minimum~~ maximum on board.

[2] Maximum Storage Devices.

Please rearrange items in ascending order of PRICE but keep the three 'SYSTEMS' sections separate as shown.

UNIT 6 Form design

At the end of Unit 6 you will have learnt how to

- *design the layout of a form using given headings/items;*
- *use different methods to allocate space on a form;*
- *use different methods of display on a form;*
- *use some of Word's desk-top publishing and drawing facilities to design a form;*
- *complete a form using preset entry points; and*
- *use the form toolbar to create and complete a simple form.*

i Form design: general hints

1 Decide whether the information which is to be inserted on the form later (by the user of the form) will be carried out by hand, on a typewriter or using a word-processing program. This will often determine the method of layout, i.e. should the allocated space take the form of dotted lines or entry points?

2 Ensure you include all headings/items given and arrange these in a logical manner. Use your initiative to design the layout, bearing in mind whether the form will be completed later by hand or machine. Make a draft plan on a piece of scrap paper first.

3 Allow suitable space after each heading/item displayed so that there is sufficient room for the relevant information to be inserted later. For example, you would need to allow more space for information on an address than you would for a date of birth.

4 Some headings may require two blocks of space to be made, for example:

   Preferred destination: Choice 1 .... Choice 2 ....

5 Follow carefully the instructions in the draft for allocating space of specified size (vertically and horizontally) for illustrations/photographs, etc. Always use a ruler afterwards to check the print-out to make sure your settings are correct.

6 Give prominence to (emphasize) specified headings/items in the form – see the section on methods of display.

7 Make good use of the paper size (i.e. don't squash everything together!) – the end result should look clear and presentable.

8 Word for Windows offers you a number of advanced form-design techniques to produce special effects such as drawing lines, shading boxes, shading paragraphs, etc. (*However, while often desirable in a business environment, these features are not essential requirements for most examinations, e.g. RSA Stage III. It would be unwise for examination candidates to spend too much time on producing unnecessary special effects for a form-design task at the expense of successfully completing other tasks.*)

Methods of display: giving prominence to form items

1 Sentences or paragraphs on the form may be emphasized by changing the **line spacing**, **insetting from the main margin** (you should inset by at least 1 inch/25 mm). To emphasize headings or items you can use **bold, underline, capitals, italics, font type** and **font size**, etc.

2 Word for Windows also gives you a number of desk-top publishing features such as the addition of **borders, lines** and **shading** around paragraphs, and also a variety of **drawing tools** – see separate instructions provided in this unit.

3 Your printer will determine which methods of display can be used as some printers are not always capable of supporting some advanced display features. Check with your tutor or printer manual and/or print a draft text copy to try out different effects.

4 However, remember the caution earlier in this unit – only use special effects in an examination when you are absolutely sure that you have completed all other tasks accurately and successfully!

Adding borders, lines, shading to headings or paragraphs

Adding borders and shading from the Borders Tool Bar

- Select: The paragraph, heading or item to which you wish to add a border and/or shading
- Click: ⊞ **Borders** button on Formatting Tool Bar:

¾ pt ――――――― ⬇	□ □ □ □ ⊞ ⊡ ⊟	□ Clear ⬇
⇑	⇑	⇑
Select a *line style* from the options shown in the line style box drop-down menu	Select type of line or border required from the *border buttons*	Select the amount of shading required from the options shown in the *shading* box drop-down menu. Shading may be applied in densities from 5 to 90 per cent, and also includes clear or solid. You can also select from a variety of fill patterns if required

Adjust the left and right margins to restrict the width of the line or border

Adding borders and shading from the menu

Select: The paragraph, heading or item

Select: **Borders and Shading** from the **Format** menu

Select: **Borders** tab – select appropriate options

Select: **Shading** tab – select appropriate options. Click: **OK**

Adjust the left and right margins to restrict the width of the line or border

Example:

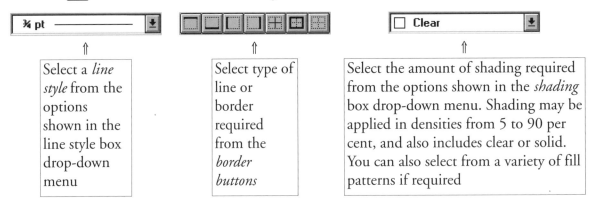

**CENTRED HEADING IN A BORDER WITH 3 PT
LINE STYLE AND 20% GREY SHADING**

Exercise 6A

6.1 To reproduce the example given, start with a clear screen and key in the following text in bold, italics and centred across the page:

CENTRED HEADING IN A BORDER WITH 3 PT LINE STYLE AND 20% GREY SHADING

6.2 Select: The whole portion of text your have just keyed in, then:

Select: **3pt** from the line style drop-down menu box

Select: The **Outside Border** button

Select: **20%** from the shading drop-down menu box

CENTRED HEADING IN A BORDER WITH 3 PT LINE STYLE AND 20% GREY SHADING

6.3 Make sure the text is still selected, then move the left margin marker to 1 inch and the right margin marker to 5 inches on the horizontal ruler.

CENTRED HEADING IN A BORDER WITH 3 PT LINE STYLE AND 20% GREY SHADING

6.4 If you wish, you can use either the shading facility or the border facility on its own:

Select: The example text again, then click on: The **No Border** icon

CENTRED HEADING IN A BORDER WITH 3 PT LINE STYLE AND 20% GREY SHADING

6.5 Close the file without saving – you do not need to print your work at this stage.

i Space allocation: dotted lines

Dotted lines are most frequently used for a form designed to be completed by hand or on a typewriter. When leaving rows of dotted lines, remember to leave one space before the first dot. It is usually good practice to end all the dotted lines at the same position. You should also use double-line spacing (or more) to allow sufficient room for the information to be inserted.

Surname . . . .

First Name . . . .

Age . . . . Date of Birth . . . .

Exercise 6B

6.6 Starting with a clear screen, prepare a telephone message form. As the finished form is designed to be completed by hand, use dotted lines for the allocation of space.

Save and print your document using filename **EX6B**. Check your print-out with that at the back of the book. If you find any errors, correct them on screen, save your document again and print again if necessary.

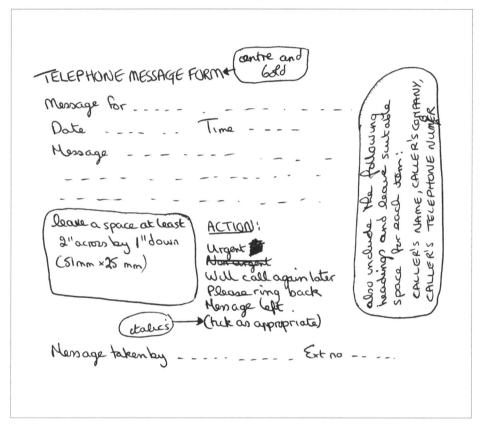

Space allocation: entry points

Entry points are usually used for a form designed to be completed later using the word-processing program to operate a command to find and replace the 'entry points'.

Entry points are simply marked (preset) points at which relevant information is to be inserted against a heading or item.

```
Surname: $

First Name: $

Address: $

Tel No: Home: $          Work: $

Age: $                    Date of Birth: $
```

After finding/searching for the entry point symbol, you should replace it with the relevant piece of information from the draft you are working from.

To use entry points in the design of the form layout

Choose a suitable symbol for the entry points which does not normally appear in the text, e.g. a *
or $. This will enable the operator who will complete the form later (by using the find/search
facility to locate the entry points and replace them with the appropriate information) to do so with
greater ease.

To complete a form which has been designed with entry points

You can either use:

- Word's **Find** command to search for the entry point symbol, then switch back to your main
  document to delete it and key in the relevant piece of information in its place. (To switch back
  temporarily to the main document, double-click the left mouse button at the entry point
  symbol – the find dialogue box remains on screen allowing you to continue the search until all
  the entry point symbols have been found); *or*

- Word's **Replace** command – use the **Find Next** box to search for the entry point symbol, and
  enter the appropriate replacement text in the **Replace With** box. Word automatically moves to
  the next occurrence of the entry point symbol – you must then delete the previous text in the
  Replace With box and re-enter the appropriate information for each entry.

Remember: If you cannot see the document text because the Find or Replace dialogue box is
covering it from view, you can use the mouse pointer to move the box to a different part of
the screen.

Look carefully at the content of the text you are presented with. It will be up to you to use your
initiative and extract the appropriate information required for insertion on to the form.

Your style of presentation should be consistent, unless it is specified otherwise.

If you are entering information which is to take up more than one line, e.g. a list of names, you
may need to set a tab in place of the entry point so that the lines begin at the same point. For
example, if the form layout shows   **Name(s): $**

- **Search for** and **delete** the $
- **Set** a left-aligned tab at the point where the $ was positioned
- **Key in** each of the names, using the tab setting to position each name on a new line.

The form will now show: **Name(s): Mohammed Sadiq**

                                          Sally Warner

                                          Gordon Sutcliffe

Exercise 6C

6.7 Starting with a clear screen, key in the form below following the layout exactly as shown and using a **$** sign to represent the entry point. Set a left-aligned tab at **2.5 inches** for the multiple-line entries.

Save and print your document using filename **EX6C**. Check your print-out with the exercise below. If you find any errors, correct them on screen, save your document again and print again if necessary.

                         J G GREENWOOD & SONS LTD
                              36 Hewitt Road
                                 Sheffield
                                 Grimsby
                                 GR3 7UR

CUSTOMER NAME: $

ADDRESS: $

TEL NO: $

JOB REF NO: $

JOB DESCRIPTION: $

JOB COMPLETED BY: $

PRICE: $ JOB COMPLETION DATE: $

PAYMENT METHOD: $ PAYMENT DATE: $

Exercise 6D

6.8 Starting with a clear screen, prepare a form for staff personnel details. As the finished form is designed to be completed using the word-processing program, use entry points for the allocation of space.

Save and print your document using filename **EX6D**. Check your print-out with that at the back of the book. If you find any errors, correct them on screen, save your document again and print again if necessary.

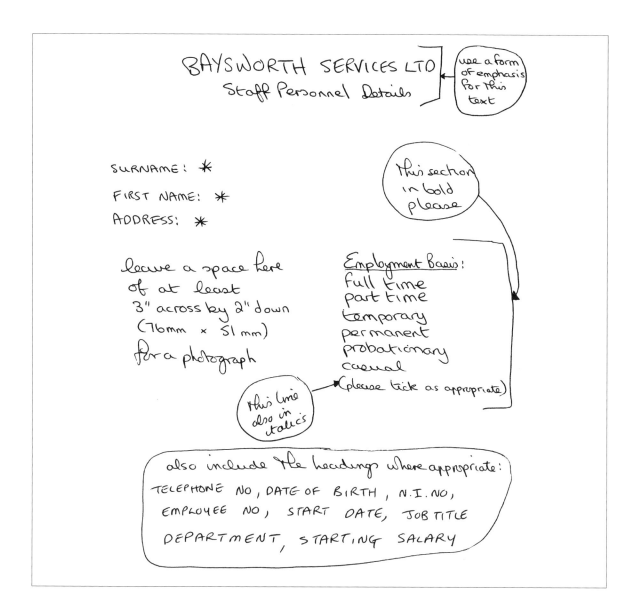

 Drawing tools

Word's drawing tools can be used to design the layout of a form in a variety of ways. You will need to familiarize yourself with the different functions of the drawing tools in order to analyse the best use for each tool in relation to the type of form being designed. Remember to consider whether the form will later be completed by hand or machine before selecting a particular drawing tool.

To show or hide the drawing toolbar

Click: on the Standard Tool Bar *or*

Select: <u>V</u>iew, <u>T</u>oolbars

A list of toolbars appears. Toolbars are toggled on or off by clicking the mouse button in the box next to each name. A toolbar is switched 'on' if there is an ✕ inside the box.

Your display should show: **✕ Drawing**

To select a drawing shape or object

Click on the drawing shape you require:

Position insertion pointer at the place you wish to start the drawing – the cursor changes to a cross-hair pointer **+**

Holding down the left mouse button, drag the shape in the appropriate direction until it is the required size

To draw a perfect circle, square or straight line, hold down the shift key while drawing the shape

To select a drawing object

Note: You *must* select a drawing object before you can edit or make any changes to it – an object is only selected when it appears with small 'handles' around it, e.g. ▐▬▌

Click: The **Select Drawing Objects** icon ▨ – the insertion pointer changes to an arrow head.

Move the arrow head to the drawing object to be selected and click the left mouse button. It is selected when small 'handles' appear around it.

To make changes to more than one drawing object, hold down the shift key while you select them all in turn. When all the objects are selected (remember, handles will appear around each one selected), release the shift key and operate the change(s) required.

To deselect a drawing object

Click: The left mouse button in an area of white space.

To resize (edit) a drawing object

You can resize a drawing object, making it either larger or smaller. You can resize it keeping the same proportions, or stretch/shrink it vertically or horizontally:

- First, select the drawing object to be edited. Then, using the mouse, point to the appropriate handle – a double-headed arrow is displayed: ↔ ↕ ↘ *or* ↗
- Click on: ↔ *or* ↕ arrow to alter the object horizontally or vertically and drag the mouse in the direction required either to increase or decrease the size
- Click on: ↘ *or* ↗ to alter the object keeping the same proportions and drag the mouse in the direction required either to increase or decrease the size

To move a drawing object

Using the mouse, point to the drawing object to be moved/repositioned. The insertion point changes to a ▨⊕

Click: The mouse pointer in the middle of the drawing object and drag it to its new position

To shade or colour a drawing object

Click on: The **Fill Color, Line Color, Line Style** icons then, select from the choices offered

To copy a drawing object

Select: The object to be copied, then operate the normal copy and paste commands

Drag the duplicate shape to the required position on the page

To cut/delete a drawing object

Select: The object to be cut/deleted, then operate the normal cut/delete commands

To group objects together

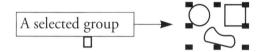

Select: The objects to be grouped (holding down the shift key):

Click on: The  **Group** icon

Any further changes will affect all the objects in the group, i.e. you may *colour, resize* or *move* them all together

To ungroup objects (previously grouped)

Select: The object group. Click on: The **Ungroup** icon

To draw a box in which you can also insert text

> This is an example of text entered into a text box. You can edit the size of the box to allow enough room for the text.

Click: the **Text Box** icon

Drag the box until it is an appropriate size for the text. Text boxes do not automatically grow if you type in more text than the original box size will allow for – you must select the text box and make it larger to make room for the extra text

Click: The insertion point inside the text box and key in the text. Text in a text box is formatted with the normal style – you can change the style of part or all the text in a text box in the same way you would reformat text in the main document

To adjust space between the text box and the text inside it:

Select: The text box

Select: **Drawing Object** from the **Format** menu

Select: **Size And Position** tab

Select or type: A value in the **Internal Margin** box. Click: **OK**

To postion a drawing object either in front or behind another object

Select: The object to be repositioned

Click: the **Bring to Front** or **Send to Back** icon

To position a drawing object either in front or behind text

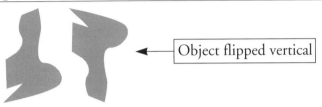

Object in fro... text   Object behind text

Select: The object to be repositioned

Click: ⬜⬜ the **Bring to Front of Text** or **Send Behind Text** icon

To flip, rotate or reshape the object

⟵ Object flipped vertical

Select: ⬜⬜⬜ the **Flip Horizontal, Flip Vertical,** *or* **Rotate Right** icon *or* ⬜ **Reshape** icon as appropriate

To 'snap' the drawing shape to an invisible network of gridlines

This can be used if you want to align drawing objects, or draw shapes with set dimensions. For example, the shapes below were drawn with identical vertical proportions by using the snap-to-grid feature:

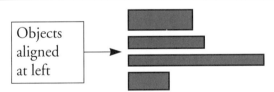

Click: ⬜ the **Snap to Grid** icon. The default spacing of gridlines is 0.1 inch but you can change both vertical and horizontal spacing between gridlines by typing or selecting a new measurement in the horizontal or vertical spacing box.

You can also change the location at which the gridlines begin (normally defaulted to start at the 0 inch point in the upper left corner of the page) on the horizontal ruler by typing or selecting a new measurement in the horizontal or vertical origin box. Gridlines are not printed.

To align drawing objects with each other

Objects aligned at left ⟶

First, select: The objects you want to align, then

Click: ⬜ the **Align Drawing Objects** icon

Select: The options you want from the **Horizontal, Vertical** and/or **Relative To** boxes. Click: **OK**

_i_   Inserting a frame

A frame can be used in order to

* position an item in a specific location;
* make text flow around an item;
* keep several items together when you move them; and
* improve the layout and appearance of an item.

You can insert an empty frame into a document in the size and position you want, and then insert text or graphics into it. Unlike a text box, a frame will automatically expand as you type more text into it. Or you can insert a frame around an existing item – Word will automatically make the frame the same size as the fixed width of the selected item.

You can edit the frame using the same commands as for the drawing tools, e.g. choose not to have a border around the frame, add different borders, shading and patterns, resize it, move it, format the text inside it, etc. As with a drawing object, the frame must be selected before it can be edited.

Unlike the text box in the drawing tools, you cannot use a frame for empty space.

To insert a frame

Select: <u>F</u>rame from the <u>I</u>nsert menu *or*

Click: Frame button on the Drawing Tool Bar

The insertion pointer changes to a cross-hair pointer **+**

Position the cross pointer where you want to start drawing the frame, hold down the left mouse button and drag the frame to required size

To delete/remove a frame

Select: The frame to be deleted/removed

Select: **Fra<u>m</u>e** from the **F<u>o</u>rmat** menu

Select: **<u>R</u>emove Frame**

Note: If you delete all the contents of a frame, the frame will also be deleted.

To specify precise measurements for the frame

Select: **Fra<u>m</u>e** from the **F<u>o</u>rmat** menu

Specify your requirement(s) in the appropriate option(s)

Exercise 6E

6.9 Starting with a clear screen, practise using Word's drawing tools and desk-top publishing facilities by

- selecting and drawing different shapes and objects, e.g. square, rectangle, circle, oval, etc.;
- enlarging and reducing the sizes of drawing shapes;
- drawing shapes using the 'snap-to-grid' feature;
- copying, moving and deleting drawing shapes;
- selecting different fill colours, line colours and line styles for the drawing shapes;
- overlapping different objects and repositioning them either in front or behind one another;
- grouping and ungrouping objects;
- aligning several objects with each other;
- inserting text into a text box; and
- inserting text into a frame.

6.10 Close the file ready for the next exercise – you do not need to save or print your work at this stage.

Exercise 6F

6.11 Starting with a clear screen, prepare a form for
TRUBRIDGE AUDIOSOUNDS LTD. The finished form is designed to be
completed by hand when it appears in several commercial publications.
The form shown below is just a sample of the type of layout which can
be produced using some of Word's desk-top publishing facilities. You
may either reproduce the example given below or, using the same
information, create a form to your own design.

Save and print your document using filename **EX6F**.

Dear Customer

We would be grateful if you could complete and return this form to us so that we may
process your order efficiently. Thank you.

Name: _____

Address: _____

_____ Postcode: _____

Telephone No: Home: _____ Work: _____

I enclose a cheque/PO: VALUE   £   :

payable to TRUBRIDGE AUDIOSOUNDS LTD

or charge my Access/VISA/Amex/Mastercard

Expiry date: _____

Signature:_____

I would like to take out the following
membership subscription with
TRUBRIDGE AUDIOSOUNDS LTD:

please tick as appropriate

☐ 6 months subscription @ £15.00

☐ 9 months subscription @ £27.50

☐ 12 months subscription @ £55.00

Exercice 6G

6.12 Starting with a clear screen, open the file **EX6C**. To complete the form use the **Find or Replace** command to find each occurrence of the $ entry point. Extract the relevant information from the letter below which is to be inserted in place of the $ entry point. (Refer to the instructions earlier in this unit, 'Space allocation: entry points'.)

Remember also if you cannot see the document text because the Find or Replace dialogue box is covering it, you may use the mouse pointer to move the box to a different part of the screen.

Save and print your document using filename **EX6G**. Check your print-out with that at the back of the book. If you find any errors, correct them on screen, save your document again and print again if necessary.

MEMORANDUM

From: *Jeff Blanchard, Foreman*

To: *Karen Hughes, Admin*

Date: *3 March 1995*

Job Ref No: 672

I am advised that repairs to Mrs Dawson's porch @ 56 Ryder Crescent, Grimsby, were completed yesterday. The estimate for the work was £325, but Jim Watmough, who completed the work, found there was some additional damage to the timbers from water leakage than was originally estimated, which added another £45 to the bill.

Mrs Dawson paid by cheque as soon as the work was completed. Jim seemed to think she was satisfied with the work but perhaps you could telephone her at home on 583356 to make sure.

Exercise 6H

6.13 Starting with a clear screen, retrieve the file EX6D and complete the form using the information given below.

Save and print your document using filename **EX6H**. Check your print-out with that at the back of the book. If you find any errors, correct them on screen, save your document again and print again if necessary.

Memorandum

From: Sue Bright, Personnel Manager, Head Office

To: Steven Ward, Personnel Manager, Leeds Branch Office

Date: 28 March 1995

STAFF APPOINTMENT

Please note that Miss Julie McNamara will be joining the staff of your Finance Department with effect from 12 April 1995 to take up the position of full time Administrative Assistant. The position is probationary for one year with a starting salary of £9,500 per annum. Can you inform payroll that Julie is employee number 697 and her national insurance number is YZ/12/89/46/A. Also, her date of birth is 26 August, 1964.

Could you please confirm the start date with Julie either by ringing her on 0532 472234 or writing to her at 27 Greenbury Road, Leeds, LS3 4DB.

Tip: You can enter the tick mark against the appropriate Employment Basis entry either:

1   by hand using a clean black pen *or*

2   using Word's insert symbol command:

Position insertion point where you want the tick to be placed:

Select: **Symbol** from the **Insert** menu

Scroll through the options in the **Font** drop-down menu box. Select: **Wingdings**

Click: The tick mark ✓ (bottom row, fourth symbol from right)

Click: **Insert, Close**

Exercise 6I

6.14 Starting with a clear screen, retrieve the file **EX6D** again and complete the form using the information given below.

Save and print your document using filename **EX6I**. Check your print-out with that at the back of the book. If you find any errors, correct them on screen, save your document again and print again if necessary.

Memorandum

From: Sue Bright, Personnel Manager, Head Office

To: Anna Price-Jones, Personnel Manager, Harrogate Branch Office

Date: 29 March 1995

STAFF APPOINTMENT

In order to assist with the current workload in your Sales department, we are to employ the clerical services of Vanessa Littlewood on a casual basis. She will be able to start the day after tomorrow and will work mornings only until further notice as employee number 698.

Her national insurance number is MB/42/73/A and her date of birth is 3 March 1959.

Can you please write to her confirming that her pay will be £3.25 per hour. Her address is 32, Hardy Avenue, Harrogate, HG4 6TE. Since Vanessa will probably be starting work with you before the letter is posted, I would suggest that you telephone her as soon as possible on 652347 to give her the information beforehand.

Exercise 6J

You can use Word to create and complete a form using the form toolbar commands. However, it is unlikely that this facility will be appropriate for examination tasks. It has been included as a basic introduction to the forms command in order to demonstrate its usefulness in the workplace. You may, therefore, choose to skip this exercise if you wish.

To create a form using Word's form fields

1 Display the Form Tool Bar on screen:

Select: **New** from the **File** menu

Click: The **Template** button. Click: **OK**

Select: **Toolbars** from the **View** menu

Click: **Forms** option to turn on the **Form Tool Bar**

2 Create a 2 column by 8 row table using the **Insert Table** icon on the Form Tool Bar. Drag the column dividing lines so that the first column is approximately 1.5 inches wide and the second column is approximately 2.5 inches wide. Merge the cells on the first row. Select the table and apply a ³/₄ point grid inside and outside border. Key in the headings for each row as shown in the example below:

STOCK ITEM	
CODE	
DESCRIPTION	
ORDER DATE	
SIZE	
COLOUR	
COST PRICE	
QUALITY APPROVED	

3 Position the insertion point in row 2, column 2, i.e. in the blank cell next to **CODE**:

Select: **Form Field** from the **Insert** menu

Click: The **Text** button in the **Type** box

Click: The **Options** button

Accept **Regular Text** from the **Type** menu box

Key in or select: **5** in the **Maximum Length** box (to limit the entry to a maximum of 5 digits)

Select: **Uppercase** from the **Text Format** box

Click: **OK**

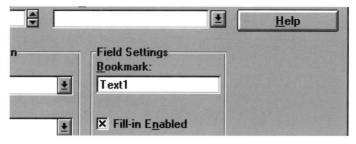

4 Position the insertion point in row 3, column 2, i.e. in the blank cell next to **DESCRIPTION**:

Click: **ab** **Text Form Field** button on the **Form Tool Bar** (this is a quick way of automatically inserting a text form field which does not require further modification)

5 Position the insertion point in row 4, column 2, i.e. in the blank cell next to **ORDER DATE**:

Select: **Insert, Form Field**

Click: **Text, Options** buttons

Select: **Date** from the **Type** menu box

Select: **dd/MM/yy** from the **Date Format** box (to set the appropriate type of date display)

Click: **OK**

6 Position the insertion point in row 5, column 2, i.e. in the blank cell next to **SIZE**:

Select: **Insert, Form Field**

Click: **Text, Options** buttons

Select: **Number** from the **Type** menu box

Key in or select: **2** in the **Maximum Length** box (to limit the entry to a maximum of 2 digits)

Select: **0** from the **Number Format** box (to set the appropriate type of number display)

Click: **OK**

7 Position insertion point in row 6, column 2, i.e. in the blank cell next to **COLOUR**:

Click: ⊞ **Drop-Down Form Field** button on the **Form Tool Bar**

Click: ⊞ **Form Field Options** button on the **Form Tool Bar**

Key in: **BLUE** in the **Drop-Down Item** box, then click: The **Add >>** button

Repeat the last step to enter the colours **RED** and **GREEN**

Click: **OK**

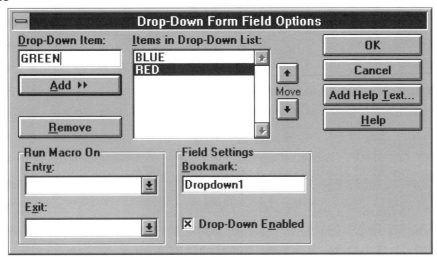

8 Position the insertion point in row 7, column 2, i.e. in the blank cell next to **COST PRICE**:

Define the entry to be **Text Form Field**, as a **Number** with a **Number Format** of **£#,##0.00** (to set the number display to currency)

Click: **OK**

9 Position the insertion point in row 8, column 2, i.e. in the blank cell next to **QUALITY APPROVED**:

Click: ⊠ **Check Box Form Field** button on the **Form Tool Bar**

Click: ⊞ **Form Field Options** button on the **Form Tool Bar**

Ensure the **Check Box Form Field Options** dialogue box shows (the check box will appear without an ✗ checkmark by default until it is entered by the operator)

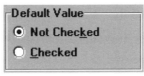

Click: **OK**

10 Your form should now appear on screen as shown below:

STOCK ITEM	
CODE	
DESCRIPTION	
ORDER DATE	
SIZE	
COLOUR	BLUE
COST PRICE	
QUALITY APPROVED	☐

11 Click: 🔒 **Protect Form** button on the Form Tool Bar to protect the form. Save the form template using filename **FORM1**. Close the template file – the new form template is ready to use.

To complete the form with data

12 To open the template form to be completed:

Select: **Open** from the **File** menu

Select: **FORM1** template and click: **OK**

Select: **Options** from the **Tools** menu and click the **Print** tab button.

Ensure that the **Update Fields** box in the printing options box is selected to ensure that the calculated field(s) are updated when the form is printed

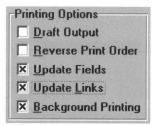

13 Click: 🅰 **Form Field Shading** button on the **Form Tool Bar** to remove the shading from the fields.

14 Key in **SW3426** for the **CODE** – Word will not allow the entry because you predetermined earlier that the maximum length for this field would be 5 digits. Edit the entry with the correct code: **SW346**. Press the tab key to move to the next field entry.

15 Key in **SWEATSHIRT** for the **DESCRIPTION**. Press the tab key to move to the next field entry.

16 Key in **26 February 1995** for the **ORDER DATE**. Press the tab key. Word automatically changes the display to match the date format display you predetermined earlier, **26/02/95**.

The date is actually incorrect. Edit the entry by keying it in as **31/02/95**. Press the tab key. Word will not accept the entry and prompts you to enter a valid time or date – this is because there are never 31 days in February! The month should be March – edit the entry again with the correct date: **31/03/95**.

17 Key in **Ten for the Size**. Press the tab key. Word will not accept the entry and prompts you to enter a valid time or date – this is because you predetermined earlier that this entry would be numerical. Edit the entry by keying it in as **10**.

18 Click on the drop-down menu arrow and select **GREEN** for the **COLOUR**.

19 Key in (£)**12.99** for the **COST PRICE**.

20 Click the check box to display an ✕ for **QUALITY APPROVED**.

21 Print the form – it should look as below:

STOCK ITEM	
CODE	SW346
DESCRIPTION	SWEATSHIRT
ORDER DATE	31/03/95
SIZE	10
COLOUR	GREEN
COST PRICE	£ 12.99
QUALITY APPROVED	⊠

22 Close the file – you do not need to save this exercise.

7 *Agendas, standard paragraphs, mailmerge*

At the end of Unit 7 you will have learnt how to

- *key in a notice and agenda for a meeting;*
- *combine standard paragraphs to create a letter;*
- *create a mailmerge form letter;*
- *create a mailmerge data source;*
- *select records from your data source;*
- *merge a data source and form letter; and*
- *view and print merged documents.*

i Notice of meeting and agenda

Notification of a meeting and the list of items to be discussed are often combined in one document. This is sent out to everyone who is entitled to attend a meeting approximately two weeks in advance of the date. The secretary of the organization or committee is responsible for the preparation of the agenda in consultation with the chairperson.

Exercise 7A

7.1 Key in the following notice and agenda.
Save as **EX7A** and print a copy of the document.

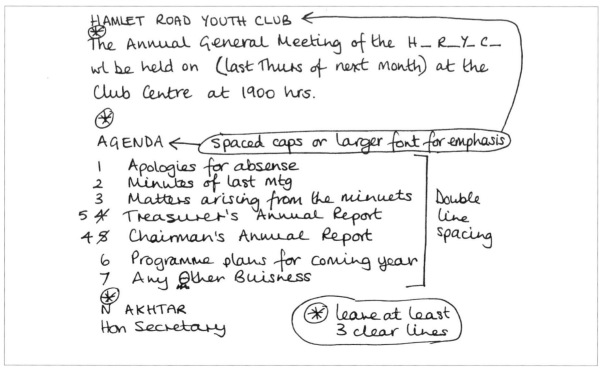

Boilerplating and standard letters

Letters and other documents used in an organization often contain sentences or paragraphs which are identical. To save time, such portions of text (or graphics) can be created once, stored and retrieved when required for insertion into documents. This may be referred to as 'boilerplating' or 'standard paragraphs'.

There are two methods of 'boilerplating' in Word:

1   saving text or graphics as individual files *or*

2   using Word's AutoText facility

Boilerplating using standard files: Method A

Store standard paragraphs as individual files:

- Key in the portion of the text to be saved as a standard paragraph file.

- Save as a separate file in the usual way by selecting **Save As** from the **File** menu, then enter an appropriate filename. (If you use easily identifiable filenames it will help you to retrieve the correct file, e.g. **SINCE** for a Yours sincerely closure, or **FAITH** for a Yours faithfully closure.)

Insert the standard paragraph file into your document:

- Position the cursor at the place where you want the standard paragraph file to be inserted.

- Retrieve the standard paragraph file by selecting **File** from the **Insert** menu, then select or key in the appropriate filename you wish to insert. Click on **OK**.

Boilerplating using AutoText: Method B

Create an AutoText entry:

- Key in the text you wish to store as a standard paragraph/item, then select (highlight) it

- Click: The [icon] **AutoText** button on the Standard Tool Bar
  or Select: **AutoText** from the **Edit** menu

The **AutoText** dialogue box appears on screen:

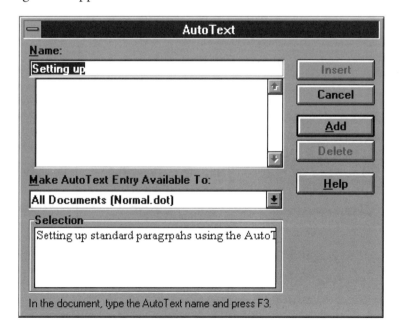

- Word suggests a name for the selection in the **N**ame box – you can overtype with a name of your own choice if you wish
- Click: The **Add** button to store the selected paragraph/item

(*Note:* You can rename, edit or delete any paragraphs in the AutoText dialogue box.)

Insert an AutoText entry:

- Position the cursor at the point you wish to insert the standard paragraph or item
- a) Type the *name* of the **AutoText** item you wish to insert

  Click: the **AutoText** button on the Standard Tool Bar *or* Press: **F3** (the item is immediately inserted into your document)

or

- b) Select: **E**dit, **AutoTe**xt from the menu and select the item you wish to insert

  Click: **F**ormatted Text button if you wish to retain any text formatting with the insertion, otherwise, click on the **P**lain Text button. Click: **I**nsert button

Exercise 7B	**7.2**	Key in the following standard paragraphs, using Method A (standard files) to store them as individual files:

Filename	Standard file text
NOTICE	A meeting of the Walton Manufacturing Co Ltd will be held on
VENUE	in the Board Room, Tunstall House, Chatsworth Lane, Chesterfield
AGENDA	A G E N D A
	1 Apologies for absence
	2 Minutes of last meeting
	3 Matters arising from minutes
AOB	Any other business
HONSEC	I J WELBECK Honorary Secretary

Exercise 7C

7.3   Create a notice and agenda from the following notes, inserting the standard paragraphs stored in Exercise 7B as indicated. Save as **EX7C** and print a copy of the document.

WALTON   MANUFACTURING LTD CO ← emphasise

Notice (15th of next month - please insert date)
Venue at ~~1130~~ +1400hrs ~~2.00 pm~~.   ✓

Agenda

4 Financial Report
5 Recruitment review
6 Review of salary scales
7 Marketing strategy

8 AOB

9 Date and time of next meeting

Hon Sec

Exercise 7D

7.4   Key in the following standard paragraphs, using Method B (AutoText) to store them as individual files:

AutoText name	AutoText entry
THANKS	Thank you for your communication of
INFO	In order to be able to deal with your complaint, we need the following information:
OFFICER	will be dealing with the matter and I can assure you that your complaint will be carefully investigated.
CLOSE	I would like to thank you for drawing our attention to this matter. It is our company policy to encourage customer feedback and we welcome the opportunity to improve our product and our service. Yours sincerely **RADFORD & MUSKHAM LTD** KATHERINE LEHRER Customer Services Manager

Exercise 7E

7.5 Create a letter from the following notes, inserting the AutoText entries stored in Exercise 7D as indicated. Save as **EX7E** and print a copy of the document.

Ref KL/CS/CPL1

Dear (leave blank for name to be inserted later)

(THANKS) (yesterday's date). I am sorry to hear that you have experienced a problem w the cooker wh you purchased from (leave space for retailer's name). [Yr letter has been passed to us for attention.

(INFO) Serial number, Model number, Date of purchase, Nature of problem. (Please set items out as a list and indent by 1" (25mm) from left margin)

James Harvester (OFFICER). He will telephone you in the immed. future to obtain the necy info.

(CLOSE)

---

i Mailmerge (or mail shot)

Mailmerge is the combining (merging) of data from two files into one file. The most common use of this feature is the production of 'personalized' letters.

The two files used to operate a mailmerge are:

1 a data file – often a list of names and addresses (this is called the 'data source' in Word); and

2 a form letter containing merge codes (marking places where information from the data file will be automatically inserted). This is called the 'form letter' in Word.

In advanced examinations you will normally be required to create one data file and one form letter. You may then be asked to select a particular cross-section of the records in the data file, and to merge these records with the form letter to produce 'individual' documents.

Note: In examinations, you may be asked to produce print-outs of the form letter and the full data file, as well as a document for each record selected from the data file.

Setting up mailmerge

The following stages should be followed:

1 Key in the text for the document.

2 Name document as 'main document'.

3 Create the data source (print if requested).

4 Insert merge codes in main document (print if requested).

5 View the merged file to check.

6 Print the merged file.

Create the main document (form letter)

The form letter contains text common to all recipients. Merge codes are inserted later to indicate the position where personalized information will be inserted from the data source.

Mouse and menu

First, key in the text for your form letter and save the document using normal save procedures. Use a suitable filename such as **MAIN1** or **MAIN2** etc.

Select: **Tools, Mail Merge**

The **Mail Merge Helper** dialogue box is displayed on screen:

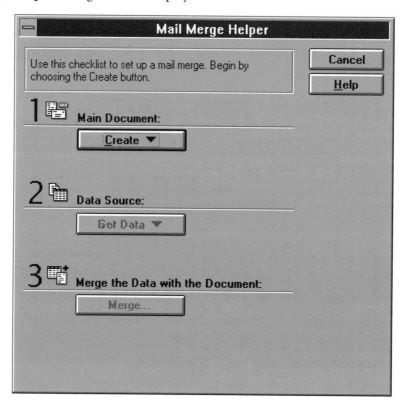

Click on: **Create** in the **Main Document** section

Select: **Form Letters** from the drop-down menu

The following dialogue box is displayed on screen:

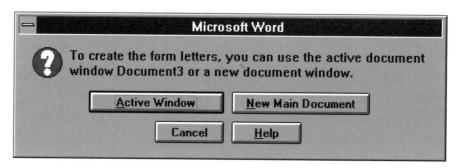

Click on: **Active Window** – the **Mail Merge Helper** dialogue box is again displayed on screen, and you are prompted to move to Section 2: Data Source

The filename for the main document form letter is displayed in Section 1.

Create the data source

The data source will contain a record for each addressee. Each record will be made up of 'fields', e.g. name, address, salutation – in other words, each field should contain the same kind of information.

Click on: **G̲et Data** in the **Data Source** section of the **Mail Merge Helper** dialogue box (2)

Select: **C̲reate Data Source** from the drop-down menu

The **Create Data Source** dialogue box is displayed on screen:

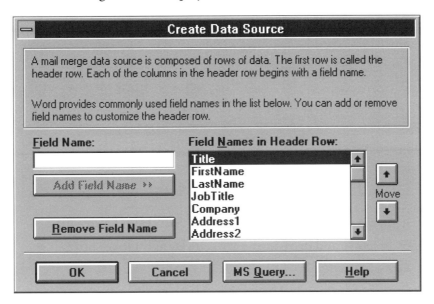

Word has already provided some commonly used field names – these are displayed in the **Field Names in Header Row** menu box. If you require a field name which is not displayed in the given list, you must *add* it to the list at this point.

To add required field names to data source:

Key in: An appropriate name for the first field in the **F̲ield Name** box (a field name must begin with a letter and must not contain spaces)

Click on: **A̲dd Field Name** to add your chosen field name to the list

Repeat until all your fields have been named and the field name added to the list

To remove unwanted field names from data source:

Select: **Field Name** not required in the **Field N̲ames in Header Row** box

Click on: **R̲emove Field Name**

Repeat until all unwanted field names are removed

Click on: **OK** to confirm field names displayed

Save the data source

The **Save Data Source** dialogue box is displayed on screen:

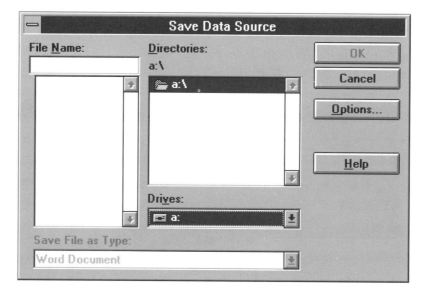

Key in: **Appropriate name** in the **File Name** box of the **Save Data Source** dialogue box

Select: **Appropriate directory and drive** in the **Directories and Drives** boxes

Click on: **OK**

The following dialogue box is displayed on screen:

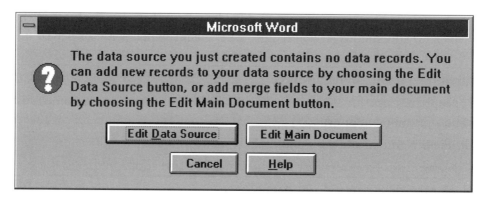

Select: **Edit Data Source** to go straight to the data form and enter the details for each record *or*

Select: **Edit Main Document** to add merge fields to the form letter

Edit the data source (enter the record details)

Click on: **Edit** **D**ata **Source**

The **Data Form** will be displayed on screen, e.g.:

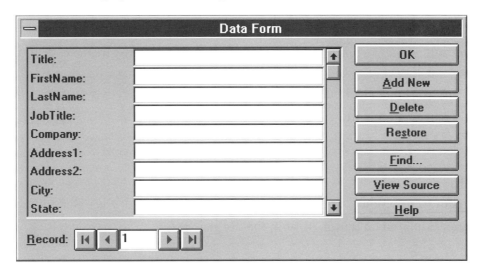

1   Key in the information for the first field and press ↵ to enter and move to next field

2   Repeat until all fields for first record are entered

3   Click on: **A**dd **New**

4   Repeat steps 1 to 3 for each record

When all records are entered, click on: **OK**

The following options are available in the data form:

Button	Action
Record	Move to another record by keying in appropriate record number *or* click on: **First Record, Previous Record, Next Record,** or **Last Record**
Delete	Deletes the current record
Restore	Reverses changes made to current record
Find	Searches for specified data throughout records
View **Source**	Displays all records in the form of a table

Print the data source

You may be required to produce a print-out of the records in your data source – at work as well as in examinations.

Click: **E**dit **Data Source** button on **Mail Merge Tool Bar** 🗗

Click: **V**iew **Source** button in **Data Form** dialogue box

(The data source file is displayed on screen in a dotted grid. You may find some of the text wraps illogically in the boxes to allow all the information to be displayed.)

Print in the normal way

Click: **Mailmerge Main Document** button on the **Mail Merge Tool Bar** to return to the main document form letter 🗗

Insert merge codes in main document

Make sure that your **Main Document Form Letter** is displayed on screen and that the **Mail Merge Tool Bar** is also on screen:

1   Move insertion pointer to position where you wish to enter the first merge code in main document
2   Click on: **Insert Merge Field** button on **Mail Merge Tool Bar**
3   Select field name required from drop-down menu
4   Repeat steps 1 to 3 for each subsequent merge field code required

Print the form letter

You may be required to produce a print-out of the form letter – at work as well as in examinations.

With form letter displayed on screen, print in the normal way.

View the merged file

In the main document window:

Click on: The **View Merged Data** button on the **Mail Merge Tool Bar**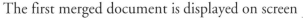

The first merged document is displayed on screen

To view other records, click on the arrow buttons ⏮ ◀ ▶ ⏭ on the **Mail Merge Tool Bar** or type the number of the required record in the box between the arrows

Print the merged file

In the main document window, click on: The **Merge to Printer** button on the **Mail Merge Tool Bar**

| **Exercise 7F** | 7.6 | Key in the following letter. Save the document (using normal save procedures) as **EX7FMAIN**. Then name it as the main document in mailmerge. (Refer to earlier instructions, 'Create the main document'.) (You may wish to use Word's automatic date format so that letters are printed with the current date.) |

Dear

GRAND RE-OPENING

I have great pleasure in enclosing an invitation to the CAPS exclusive preview of our refurbished store. [You may have noticed that extensive alterations have been taking place recently and we wd like you and yr family as members to be among the first to enjoy a totally new shopping exp. // I look forward to welcoming you.

Yrs scly

Marketing Manager

7.7 With the Mailmerge helper dialogue box on screen, refer to earlier instructions, 'Create the data source', and create a data source file, using the following field names: **Title, First Name, Last Name, Address1, Address2, City, PostalCode, Membership**. (All these field names are already provided in Word's field names list, apart from membership, which you will need to *add* to the list.)

Save the data source as **EX7FDATA**.

7.8 Referring to the earlier instructions, 'Edit the data source', enter the following data into the data form (three records). (Enter the initials in the first name field.)

Mrs P Agarwal
17 High Lane
Listerton
DENBRIDGE
DE10 2DI
VIP

Mr W T Beechill
Clevely House
Roundhill
LUNDLEY
LY3 3RJ
VIP

Dr M Ullah
Moorside
Rapley Green
ANWORTH
AH11 2HM
Star

⌐ULLAH⌐

7.9 Refer to the earlier instructions, 'Print the data source', and print a copy of the records you have just added as your data source.

7.10 Referring to the earlier instructions, 'Insert merge codes in main document', insert merge codes into the main document as shown below. (Leave a space between fields where appropriate.)

« Title » « First Name » « Last Name »
« Address1 »
« Address2 »
« City »
« PostalCode »

Dear « Title » « LastName »
I have great pleasure ... your family as
« Membership » members to be ...

7.11 Save the form letter including merge codes using the same filename **EX7FMAIN**. Print a copy of the form letter showing the merge codes (see example below):

Date of typing

«Title» «FirstName» «LastName»
«Address1»
«Address2»
«City»
«PostalCode»

Dear «Title» «LastName»

GRAND RE-OPENING

I have great pleasure in enclosing an invitation to the Exclusive Preview of our refurbished store.

You may have noticed that extensive alterations have been taking place recently and we would like you and your family as «Membership» members to be among the first to enjoy a totally new shopping experience.

I look forward to welcoming you.

Yours sincerely

Marketing Manager

Enc

7.12 View the merged file to check the documents.

7.13 Save the merged file using filename **EX7FMERG** and print the merged file.

Exercise 7G

7.14 Add the following two records to the data source (edit data source). Ensure that the data form is clear before adding new records.

Miss G M O'Dowd
146 Willow Cres
Langford
JAMESTOWN
JN7 8AL
Star

Mrs K Clare
25 Second Ave
Crofton
NUTFIELD
ND4 3DN
VIP

7.15 Save the amended data source using filename **EX7GDATA** and print a copy of the updated data source.

Select specific records to be merged

You may be requested to merge a form letter with a selection of the data source records which match specific criteria.

After inserting merge codes in the main document:

Click: The **Mail Merge Helper** button on the **Mail Merge Tool Bar**

Click: **Query Options** button in Section 3

Select: The appropriate field from the drop-down menu in the **Field** box

Select: **Equal to** from the drop-down menu in the **Comparison** box

Key in: The required criterion in the **Compare To** box

Click: **OK**

Close: **Mail Merge Helper** dialogue box

View the merged file to check selection before printing (the number of selected records is displayed on the **Mail Merge Tool Bar**)

Save the merged file

7.16 Merge the form letter with the records for **VIP** members only.

7.17 View the merged file to check the documents.

7.18 Save the merged file using filename **EX7GMERG** and print the merged file.

Exercise 7H

7.19 Open the file saved as **EX7E** and use it as the main document for a mailmerge. Save as **EX7HMAIN.**

7.20 Create a data source from the following information and print a copy. Use the field names **Title, FirstName, LastName, Address1, Address2, City, PostalCode, Retailer**. Save as **EX7HDATA**.

Mr & Mrs RP Jarvis
Churchfield
21 Church Lane
HOLMEVILLE
HE1 7RL
Gregson & Waite Ltd

Mr B Surley
27 Orchard Way
Hammerfield
LONGLAND
LD8 8DH
Gregson & Waite Ltd

Miss Shazia Hasan
37 Grange Court
Worthwood
NORTONBURY
NY5 42X
Euro Electrics PLC

Mr T Knapp
Eastfield Manor
Eastfield
WHERTON
WN11 7NR
Euro E____ PLC

Mrs Pauline Moran
10 Emsley Pk Drve
Emsley
NORTONBURY
NY3 6MJ
E____ E____ PLC

Ms Susannah Bruno
Dean Hill
Vernon Rd
WHERTON
WN9 3JS
G___ & W_ Ltd

Mr and Mrs J F Spencer
12 Windsor Ct
Hammerfield
LONGLAND
LD8 7SU
G & W Ltd

Mr I J Royd
16 James St
Vale Moor
LOW CROFT
LT6 9FC
E_E_ PLC

Mrs L A Wachewska
Oak House
Mount
ALLANTON
AN8 6PJ
Gregson & Waite Ltd

Mr Thomas Van-Helf
10 Dodgson Ave
Dene Green
CAMTON
CN4 3MA
G & W_Ltd

7.21 Insert merge codes into the form letter using the relevant field names in the appropriate positions in the letter. Save as **EX7HMAIN** (replacing previous document) and print a copy of the form letter showing the merge codes.

7.22 Merge the form letter and the data source, selecting only Gregson & Waite's customers.

7.23 View to check and then print the merged file. Save as **EX7HMERG**.

UNIT 8

Consolidation 2

Exercise 8A **Part 1** Please prepare this application booking form. Since it is designed to be completed by hand, use Word's drawing and desk-top publishing facilities to produce an appropriate layout.

Change the word **Fernfield** to **Ferndale** wherever it occurs in Exercise 8A, Parts 1 and 2, and the next exercise, Exercise 8B.

Save and print your document using filename **EX8A1**. Check your print-out with that at the back of the book. Your chosen layout may not be identical with the example print-out check provided, but ensure that you have included all the relevant information. If you find any errors, correct them on screen, save your document again and print again if necessary.

FERNFIELD THEATRE BOOKING FORM ← (centre and emphasise)

Name: _____

Address: _____

_____ Postcode: _____

Telephone: day: _____ evening: _____

I wish to make the following booking:

(Include the headings: Production, Date, ~~Time~~
Venue, No of tickets, Ticket price
leaving appropriate space for each one.)

Payment Method (please tick as appropriate):

☐ A) I authorise you to debit my Access/Visa account
number (delete as appropriate):

_____

Expiry date: _____ Signed: _____

☐ B) I enclose a Cheque/Postal Order for the total
amount made payable to Fernfield Council.

Please complete and return with payment to:
Fernfield Theatre Box Office
27-29 Reighton Rd
FERNFIELD
F07 4AG

(use a form of
emphasis for all
lines of text.
underlined with ∿∿∿)

Exercise 8A **Part 2** Prepare another form which will allow you to transfer

the written information from the form you designed in the previous
exercise to a computer. Include the given headings where appropriate
and allow sufficient space for each item inserting a symbol such as a *
or @ at infil points.

Save and print your document using filename **EX8A2**. Check your print-
out with that at the back of the book. Your chosen layout may not be
identical with the example print-out check provided, but ensure that
you have included all the relevant information. If you find any errors,
correct them on screen, save your document again and print again if
necessary.

FERNFIELD THEATRE BOOKING FORM ← (centre + bold)

Name : @

Address : @

Postcode : @

Telephone : day : @   evening : @

(leave at least ½" (13mm) before and after this section)

Method of payment : @

(indent ½" (13mm) at left margin)

If paying by Visa or Access : Credit card/number : @

Expiry date of credit card : @

Customer signature obtained (enter YES or NO) : @

(Include the headings : Production, Venue, Date, No of tickets, Ticket price, Total payment)

(put text underlined with ~~~ in italic)

Exercise 8B

Prepare this table, using the paper with the shorter edge at the top. Rearrange the productions in ascending **DATE** order but keeping the October and November sections separate as shown.

Save and print your document using filename **EX8B**. Check your print-out with that at the back of the book. If you find any errors, correct them on screen, save your document again and print again if necessary.

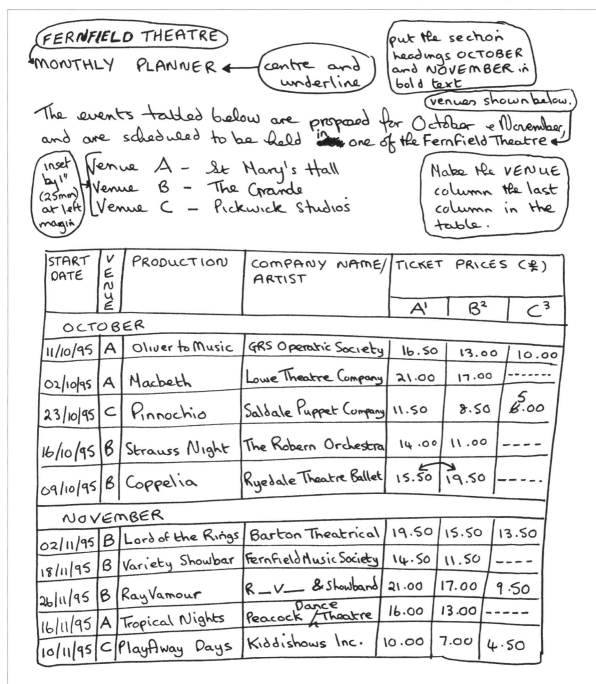

(FERNFIELD THEATRE)

MONTHLY PLANNER ← centre and underline

put the section headings OCTOBER and NOVEMBER in bold text

The events tabled below are proposed for October & November, and are scheduled to be held in one of the Fernfield Theatre venues shown below.

inset by 1" (25mm) at left margin

Venue A - St Mary's Hall
Venue B - The Grande
Venue C - Pickwick Studios

Make the VENUE column the last column in the table.

START DATE	VENUE	PRODUCTION	COMPANY NAME/ARTIST	TICKET PRICES (£)		
				A[1]	B[2]	C[3]
OCTOBER						
11/10/95	A	Oliver to Music	GRS Operatic Society	16.50	13.00	10.00
02/10/95	A	Macbeth	Lowe Theatre Company	21.00	17.00	-------
23/10/95	C	Pinnochio	Saldale Puppet Company	11.50	8.50	5.00
16/10/95	B	Strauss Night	The Robern Orchestra	14.00	11.00	----
09/10/95	B	Coppelia	Ryedale Theatre Ballet	15.50	19.50	-----
NOVEMBER						
02/11/95	B	Lord of the Rings	Barton Theatrical	19.50	15.50	13.50
18/11/95	B	Variety Showbar	Fernfield Music Society	14.50	11.50	----
26/11/95	B	Ray Vamour	R_V_ & Showband	21.00	17.00	9.50
16/11/95	A	Tropical Nights	Peacock Dance Theatre	16.00	13.00	-----
10/11/95	C	PlayAway Days	Kiddishows Inc.	10.00	7.00	4.50

[1] Friday and Saturday evenings - 20% discounts for Children, Students, Over 60s.

[2] Tues - Thurs evenings - 30 per cent discounts for Children, Students, Over 60s

[3] Matinees only - no ~~discounts~~ discounts available.

Exercise 8C

Please set up and print a data file with these
ten records

Ms Rachel Coombes
24 Barber Cr
Leighton
CRAGLAND
CD5 6PJ   (Ordinary)

Mr & Mrs C Janes
Kingston House
Stoneley
STONEFORD
SD11 6JM
Concessionary

Ms Louisa Deneve
146 Long Rd
Burkiston
BELLWOOD
BW7 3MO
                          } ordinary

Mrs G Dziaszyk
Easter Cottage
Easter Lane
CRAGLAND
CD4 3NT

Mr T Heine
6 Feltham Gr
Burkiston
BELLWOOD
BW3 6MJ
Concessionary

Miss Rebecca Martyn
160 Westland Ave
Top Scarr
SCAR HILL
SC22 4FG
Concessionary

Rev PW Wright
The Vicarage
Oakley
STONEFORD
SD7 8VG
Ordinary

Dr Peter Anstruther
Margaret's House
Lady Rd
ROYDLEY
RO8 4PB

Mr & Mrs Johann Pesendorfer
16 Lake View Terr
Lakeside
LOUGHTON
LN8 6PW   } Concessionary

Miss Esther Beckett
1 May Green
Top Scarr
SCAR HILL
SC20 6LH

Please note: 'ordinary' and
'concessionary' refer to membership types.
You may, therefore, use the field name: membership
when setting up the data file for this field

(Please send this letter to all the concessionary members)

Ref FT/MS/AS070

(Please print a copy of the letter showing merge codes for the file.)

*
*
*
*
*

Dear * *

~~MEMBERSHIP~~ AUTUMN SEASON ← *(emphasise)*

Our new Autumn program offers something for everyone from Shakespeare and Strauss to Vaudeville and Pinocchio. There's a special fun-packed show for the children where ↑ participation ~~by the~~ (audience) is not just encouraged, it's ~~welcomed~~!
                                                          expected

As a * subscription member~~ship~~, you can take advantage of reduced prices and priority booking.

(Our monthly planner and booking form are enclosed, together with the Autumn programme brochure. Enjoy browsing thro' the brochure but don't take too long! Return your b— f— asap to ensure the dates and seats you require.

Happy theatre-going!

Yrs scly   *(Ragged R margin please)*

Judith O'Conner
BOX OFFICE MANAGER

DISTANT LANDS

Exotic holidays in faraway places

126-128 Orient Road Fartown
KIRKDALE KE6 8IL

Tel: 0448-765431

❖❖❖

PORTALS LTD

**Quality garage
and house doors
Established 1929**

Unit 10
Highfields Business Park
YORK YO6 8YH

Tel: 987669 Fax: 986786

NATIONAL MOTOR AND TRAVEL ASSOCIATION

Automobile House, Crossroads Way,
BRADFORD, BD10 5XC
Tel: 01274-664332 Fax: 01274-233466

Security and
care wherever
you go

Print-out checks

**NATIONAL MOTOR AND
TRAVEL ASSOCIATION**
**Automobile House, Crossroads Way,
BRADFORD, BD10 5XC**
Tel: 01274-664332 Fax: 01274-233466

*Security and
care wherever
you go*

Date of typing

URGENT

Mrs L Porter
The Coach House
Station Road
Oxenwood
KEIGHLEY
West Yorkshire
BD22 4CH

Dear Mrs Porter

ROADSAFE PLAN

You have recently made enquiries about our new ROADSAFE PLAN which is currently being offered to long-standing, valued customers such as yourself. I enclose a leaflet giving full details, together with an application form.

The insurance plan gives additional cover to that which you already receive under our existing scheme and as you are already a member of our organisation, there will be no need for you to take a medical examination. You will automatically be accepted on to the ROADSAFE PLAN provided you live in England, Wales, Scotland, the Channel Islands or the Isle of Man.

It is an unfortunate fact that if you are injured whilst travelling, you may be off work for some time. You may even be unable to continue in your former occupation but the bills will still have to be paid!

As well as being covered for accidents in your own vehicle, you will also be covered whilst travelling in someone else's car as a passenger. The plan extends to world-wide pedestrian and passenger/public transport travel for the insured. Motor-cyclists are covered under our 'Wings' scheme.

Please consider the attached leaflet over the next 7 days. Simply select the type of cover you require, complete the application form and return it to us in the envelope provided. You will receive your policy within 4 days and you may then read and study it thoroughly before committing yourself.

We look forward to hearing from you in the near future.

Yours sincerely
NATIONAL MOTOR AND TRAVEL ASSOCIATION

A B AXLEFORD
Customer Services Officer

Encs

You're late! We've been waiting for you. Sit down and we'll start or there'll be no food left for you.

Don't say you can't do the work. It's not difficult and there's no reason why you shouldn't finish it.

The sun's glare caused the player's eyes to lose sight of his opponent's ball. The game's end was announced and the winner's victory was acknowledged by the other team's captain.

The city's streets were crowded as tourists and residents waited to see the Mayor's car arrive at the entrance to the Club. The Freedom of the City was to be bestowed on the city's football team and its manager.

It's your decision as to whether you wish to bring the dog on Saturday. It's well-behaved and the children like its friendly nature. They were pleased to hear that it's recovered from its recent illness and they are looking forward to its coming so that it can play with its new toys and they can see for themselves that it's fit and well again.

We were always told to be careful to dot our i's and cross our t's but the typewriter, which must date from the 1950's or 1960's, wouldn't print w's and p's and missed the tails off the y's, q's and g's!

Exercise 1C

PORTALS LTD

Unit 10
Highfields Business Park
YORK YO6 8YH

**Quality garage
and house doors
Established 1929**

Tel: 987669 Fax: 986786

Our ref 95/10/GDENQ

Date of typing

FOR THE ATTENTION OF MR B N FREE

Hermann & Free Ltd
210-216 Larches Road
Whiteacre Park
LEEDS
LS26 3FX

Dear Sirs

<u>PORTALS GARAGE DOORS</u>

Further to your telephone enquiry of *(yesterday's date)*, I have pleasure in sending you copies of our colour brochures illustrating our full product range. An up-to-date trade price list is also enclosed.

Doors are manufactured in timber, steel or GRP (moulded fibreglass) in a wide variety of finishes. A choice of door operation is provided: canopy, tracked and non-protruding. Full performance tests are carried out after installation and materials are tested for durability. Consistency is ensured by manufacturing methods supported by BS5750 standards.

The security aspect is not overlooked. We realize that many householders use their garage for the storage of valued and valuable items such as bicycles and gardening equipment, and we have paid special attention to locking systems. All of our doors are supplied with a high security system as standard. Remote control operation is increasingly popular and is available as part of our range.

We feel that the selection of garage doors to suit the house style and local environment is an important factor in providing a quality home and we are sure you will find a style which will enhance your new development at Rose Dell.

You may be interested to know that our new showroom will be opened on *(next Saturday's date)* in Unit 10 at the Highfields Business Park. The opening ceremony will take place at 12 noon and will be followed by refreshments. I have pleasure in enclosing 8 VIP invitation vouchers for the use of members of your firm.

A PRIZE DRAW is planned and the winner will receive a weekend break for 2 at the 'Leisuretime' hotel of their choice. Additional prizes will include meals at the Lotus Garden restaurant and tickets for performances at York's Grand Theatre. I hope that you can attend our showroom opening and look forward to meeting you.

Exercise 1B

PORTALS LTD

Unit 10
Highfields Business Park
YORK YO6 8YH

**Quality garage
and house doors
Established 1929**

Tel: 987669 Fax: 986786

Our ref 95/10/GDENQ

Date of typing

FOR THE ATTENTION OF MR B N FREE

Hermann & Free Ltd
210-216 Larches Road
Whiteacre Park
LEEDS
LS26 3FX

Dear Sirs

<u>PORTALS GARAGE DOORS</u>

Further to your telephone enquiry of *(yesterday's date)*, I have pleasure in sending you copies of our colour brochures illustrating our full product range. An up-to-date trade price list is also enclosed.

Doors are manufactured in timber, steel or GRP (moulded fibreglass) in a **wide variety of** finishes. A choice of door operation is provided: canopy, tracked and non-protruding. Full performance tests are carried out after installation and materials are tested for durability. Consistency is ensured by manufacturing methods supported by BS5750 standards.

The security aspect is not overlooked. We realize that many householders use their garage for the storage of valued and valuable items such as bicycles and gardening equipment, and we have paid special attention to locking systems. All of our doors are supplied with a high security system as standard. Remote control operation is increasingly popular and is available as part of our range.

We feel that the selection of garage doors to suit the house style and local environment is an important factor in providing a quality home and we are sure you will find a style which will enhance your new development at Rose Dell.

Please contact me if you require further *information. The usual trade terms and conditions* apply. As you requested, I am sending a copy of this letter and copies of brochures to your Sheffield Office for the attention of Mr S Driver. I hope that he will be impressed by the service we can provide.

I look forward to furthering our business association.

Yours sincerely

N GATESBY
Sales Manager

Encs

Copy to Mr S Driver, Hermann & Free Ltd, Sheffield Office

Exercise 2A

NATIONAL MOTOR AND TRAVEL ASSOCIATION

ROADSAFE PLAN

Apply Now!

Don't leave it too late. Apply to join our new Roadsafe Plan today! Complete the Application Form within the next 7 days and take advantage of our special introductory offer. Your policy will be with you within 4 days and you then have 14 days in which to study the plan before you finally commit yourself. Post your application in the pre-paid envelope.

Introductory Offer

As soon as we receive the payment of your first premium, we will send you a stylish Clock Radio with our compliments. If you decide to adopt the new Roadsafe Plan within 7 days of receiving your policy, you will also receive a beautiful writing set containing a classic black onyx NMTA fountain pen and ball-point pen. These valuable items would cost at least £30 in the high street shops.

The Benefits

If you have an accident whilst travelling and you are off work for at least 10 consecutive working days, you will receive £90 per week for up to 2 years.

If you were fatally injured whilst travelling, your estate would receive a substantial cash payment of £100,000.

Adults aged under 25 and over 65 receive 60% of the benefits; children 25%. At each renewal date, the premium increases automatically by 5% but we guarantee that you will not be asked to pay a higher premium however many claims you make.

1

Exercise 1C (cont.)

Please contact me if you require further information. The usual trade terms and conditions apply. As you requested, I am sending a copy of this letter and copies of brochures to your Sheffield Office for the attention of Mr S Driver. I hope that he will be impressed by the service we can provide.

I look forward to furthering our business association.

Yours sincerely

N GATESBY
Sales Manager

Encs

Copy to Mr S Driver, Hermann & Free Ltd, Sheffield Office

2

Exercise 2B

LEISURETIME HOTELS

Countryside and Countrywide Weekend Breaks

Whether you want to unwind in the peace of the countryside, live it up in the capital or visit places of interest, Leisuretime Hotels can offer you the perfect solution. With over 200 hotels, there's sure to be one which is just right for you.

Your Hotel

You can be sure of a warm welcome and great service. All rooms have a private bathroom and you will be served a full English breakfast every morning. Tea and coffee making facilities are available in all rooms. Colour TV is provided in all hotel rooms.

Your Family

Children sharing a room with adults in a 3 or 4-bedded room stay FREE. Under 5 years of age, children may eat FREE. If you are taking a weekend break for 3 nights, 2 children under 15 may have a FREE room! (Babysitting services are usually available if booked in advance.) Full details of other special FREE offers are shown on Page 10 of the current brochure.

Midweek Breaks

If you can manage to get away during the week, you can miss the traffic jams and the crowds! You may stay for 2 or more consecutive nights between Monday and Thursday for only £50 per person per night. Dinner, bed and breakfast are included in the price.

1

Exercise 2A (cont.)

Extra Cover

Not only will you and your family be covered for accidents in your own vehicle, you will also be covered as a passenger in someone else's car. Should you be injured by a motor vehicle as a pedestrian, you are also covered. Any fare-paying public transport, anywhere in the world, is included in the plan.

Lump Sum Payments

A lump sum of £120,000 is payable if you permanently lose the use of 2 limbs or the sight in both eyes. £60,000 is payable for the loss of the use of 1 limb or the sight in 1 eye.

Daily and Weekly Payments

You may be paid £90 per day if you have to spend time in hospital as an in-patient. The maximum time for this payment is 365 consecutive days.

You may be paid £110 per week if you are unable to continue with your normal occupation for at least 2 weeks. This benefit is payable for a minimum of 3 weeks and a maximum of 18 months.

Guaranteed Cover

If you are eligible (over the age of 21 and a NMTA member), your acceptance onto the Roadsafe Plan is guaranteed.

JUST COMPLETE THE FORM AND POST IT TODAY!

2

Exercise 3A

NMTA PLAN

NATIONAL MOTOR AND TRAVEL ASSOCIATION

ROADWISE PLAN

APPLY NOW!

Don't leave it too late. Apply to join our new Roadwise Plan as soon as possible! Complete the Application Form within the next 14 days and take advantage of our special introductory offer - this offer is available for a limited period only. Your policy will be sent to you within 4 days and you then have 21 days in which to study the plan before you finally commit yourself. Just complete the form and post it as soon as possible!

INTRODUCTORY OFFER

As soon as we receive the payment of your first premium, we will send you a stylish Clock Radio with our compliments.

If you decide to adopt the new Roadwise Plan within 14 days of receiving your policy, you will also receive a beautiful writing set containing a classic silver-plated NMTA fountain pen and ball-point pen. These valuable items would normally cost at least £30 in the high street shops.

Exercise 2B (cont.)

Weekend Budget Breaks at selected hotels

Stay for 2 or more nights and choose from bed and breakfast, or dinner, bed and breakfast. Prices start from only £30 per person per night.

If you can manage to get away for only 1 night, perhaps after visiting an exhibition or attending a function, we will be pleased to accommodate you. Special 1-night breaks are available on Fridays or Saturdays only. The price is the same - £30 per person per night.

Touring Breaks

Our unique voucher system means that you can travel by car and stay for 1 or 2 nights at one hotel and then drive to another hotel for the third (and fourth) night. Accommodation is at certain participating hotels which offer the same high standards of service as all of our hotels. The maximum stay in any hotel is 2 nights.

Plan your route and tell us where you'd like to stay. We'll pre-book your hotels for you and save you the worry. You'll know that a warm welcome and a 3-course dinner will be waiting for you at the end of a hard day's sightseeing!

Coach and Rail Breaks

Let someone else worry about the driving. Relax and admire the countryside as you travel to your chosen hotel. Our Booking Service staff will be able to advise you on the best route and the quickest method of travel.

Booking Service

You can ring us for the cost of a local call at any time. The Service operates 24 hours a day. Our advisers will help you to make the best selection at the best price. Ring us on 01425-861-610 today.

2

Exercise 3A (cont.)

NMTA PLAN

DAILY, WEEKLY AND LUMP SUM PAYMENTS

Whether you are involved in an accident or lose your job, the bills will still keep coming in!

a) You may be paid **£40 per day** if you have to spend time in hospital as an in-patient. The maximum time for this payment is **365 consecutive days.**

b) You may be paid **£110 per week** if you are unable to continue with your normal occupation for at least 2 weeks. This benefit is payable for a minimum of 3 weeks and a maximum of 18 months.

c) A lump sum of **£120,000** is payable if you permanently lose the use of 2 limbs or the sight in both eyes. **£60,000** is payable for the loss of the use of 1 limb or the sight in 1 eye.

Just complete the form and post it as soon as possible!

Exercise 3A (cont.)

NMTA PLAN

GUARANTEED COVER

If you are eligible (over the age of 21 and a NMTA member) your acceptance onto the Roadwise Plan is guaranteed. You won't have to take a medical or even answer questions about your health.

THE BENEFITS

If you were fatally injured whilst travelling, your estate would receive a cash payment of £100,000.

If you have an accident whilst travelling and you are off work for at least 10 consecutive working days, you will receive £90 per week for up to 2 years.

Adults aged under 25 and over 65 receive 60% of the benefits; children 25%. At each renewal date, the premium increases automatically by 5% but we guarantee that you will not be asked to pay a higher premium however many claims you make.

EXTRA COVER

Not only will you and your family be covered for accidents in your own vehicle, you will also be covered if you are a passenger in someone else's car, or if you are involved in an accident as a pedestrian.

Any fare-paying public transport, anywhere in the world, is included in the plan, including:

a) taxis and buses

b) trains

c) ships

d) ferry boats

e) hovercraft

f) aeroplanes

Accidents on a motor bike are excluded but motor cyclists can be covered with the NMTA Wheels Scheme.

Exercise 3B (cont.)

JOYWAYS

Weekend Budget Breaks

If you can manage to get away for only 1 night, perhaps after visiting an exhibition or attending a function, we will be pleased to accommodate you. Special 1-night breaks are available on Fridays or Saturdays only. The price is £30 per person per night.

Stay for 2 or more nights and choose from bed and breakfast, or dinner, bed and breakfast. Prices start from only £30 per person per night.

Midweek Breaks

If you can manage to get away during the week, you can miss the traffic jams and the crowds! You may stay for 2 or more consecutive nights between Monday and Thursday for only £45 per person per night. Dinner, bed and breakfast are included in the price.

Exercise 3B

JOYWAYS

JOYWAYS HOTELS

Get-Away with JoyWays

You can feel confident when you book your JoyWays break. There are no hidden extras. Part of our great value package is our "Privilege Voucher Pack" - a book of discount vouchers giving you special discounts on admission to exciting local attractions. Ring us on 01425-861-610 today.

Countryside and Countrywide Weekend Breaks

Whether you want to unwind in the peace of the countryside, live it up in the capital or visit places of interest, JoyWays Hotels can offer you the perfect solution.

Choose from the bright lights and sights of a big city, the architecture, traditional character and heritage of an historic town, the forrested fells and mountain peaks of the Lakes and Highlands, or the rolling countryside of a charming country village. With over 200 hotels, there's sure to be one which is just right for you.

Your Hotel

You can be sure of great service and a warm welcome. All rooms have a private bathroom and you will be served a full traditional English breakfast every morning. Tea and coffee making facilities are available in all rooms except where indicated. Colour TV is provided in all hotel rooms. On half-board breaks, 3-course table d'hôte dinner with coffee or your choice of 3 courses from each Hotel's own "Specialité Menu".

Your Family

Family fun begins when every child is given a FREE JoyWays Fun Pack to keep them amused whilst you unpack. JoyWays Hotels have a great deal to offer cost-conscious families, with many money saving offers also available during school holidays:

a) Most Hotels offer a FREE baby-listening service.

b) Cots, highchairs and FREE baby food are available on request.

c) Children sharing a room with adults in a 3 or 4-bedded room stay FREE.

d) Under 5 years of age, children may eat FREE.

e) On a 3-night weekend break 2 children under 15 may have a FREE room!

Full details of many more special FREE offers are shown on Page 12 of the current brochure.

Unit 4 Task 1

DISTANT LANDS
Exotic holidays in faraway places

126-128 Orient Road Fartown
KIRKDALE KE6 8IL
❖❖❖❖❖❖❖❖❖❖❖❖❖❖❖❖❖❖❖

Tel: 0448-765431

❖❖❖❖❖❖❖❖❖❖❖❖❖❖❖❖❖❖❖

Today's date

PERSONAL

Mr & Mrs F T Sandal
West Lodge
St Clement's Avenue
Trimmington
ROCHLEY
RY12 1AG

Dear Mr & Mrs Sandal

DISTANT LANDS HOLIDAY OPPORTUNITY OF A LIFETIME!

As a valued customer of our sister company, 'Holiday Dreams', I would like to offer you the privilege of previewing our new holiday brochure for the coming season before its release to the general public.

Distant Lands holidays, as suggested by the name, cover destinations world-wide while maintaining the same high standards and competitive prices as 'Holiday Dreams'. We can transport you west to the Caribbean or to Thailand in the Far East, with many other destinations in between such as Africa, Egypt and India.

Our special introductory offer to you is available until *(last day of month after next)*. All you have to do is to select the holiday of your choice from the enclosed brochure. When you have confirmed your booking through your travel agent, you will save up to £100 per person on a 14-night holiday.

For the 'young at heart', a romantic wedding, honeymoon or 'second honeymoon' in a perfect setting can be arranged for destinations in the Caribbean, Sri Lanka and Goa on India's west coast. Leave all the wedding details to our staff - they will make all the necessary arrangements including the marriage licence, and will ensure a beautiful setting for your special day. Our 'Romance in Distant Lands' video can be purchased for £7.99 - see how your dream could come true!

The honeymoon service begins with a bottle of champagne on your outward flight and ends with a candlelit dinner on the last evening at your holiday hotel.

As you will see from the enclosed **Distant Lands** brochure, we offer superb deals for families with reductions from 10% for all 2-11 year olds and 50% for the first child. Infants of 0-2 years can travel for only £75. (They will not be served food and are expected to sit on a parent's knee during the flight.) Group reductions are available for 15 or more full-fare paying passengers, and self-catering accommodation offers savings for the third and fourth adult sharing a room.

Exercise 3B (cont.)

JOYWAYS

Touring Breaks

Our unique voucher system means that you can travel by car and stay for 1 or 2 nights at one hotel and then drive to another hotel for the third (and fourth) night. Accommodation is at certain participating hotels which offer the same high standards of service as all of our hotels. The maximum stay in any hotel is 2 nights.

Plan your route and tell us where you'd like to stay. We'll pre-book your hotels for you and save you the worry. You'll know that a warm welcome and a 3-course dinner will be waiting for you at the end of a hard day's sightseeing!

Coach and Rail Breaks

Let someone else worry about the driving. Relax and admire the countryside and scenery as you travel to your chosen hotel. Our Booking Service staff will be able to advise you on the best route and the most appropriate method of travel.

Booking Service

You can ring us for the cost of a local call at any time. The Service operates 24 hours a day. Our advisers will help you to make the best selection at the best price.

Ring us on 01425-861-810 today.

REF/JB/Flyer

8

Unit 4 Task 2

GENERAL GUIDELINES

Choosing your perfect holiday is part of the pleasure of the whole experience. However, you should choose with care to ensure full enjoyment.

MAKING AN INFORMED CHOICE

Read the details in the brochure carefully. The information will be accurate but, for example, you cannot afford to miss the fact that a hotel's access to the beach is by steep steps if you have infants or disabled persons in your party. Ask your agent for further details of your choice before booking.

PASSPORTS AND VISAS

British visitors passports are not valid for all destinations. Allow yourself sufficient time to obtain a full passport. Some countries also require a visa. Check with your travel agent and relevant embassies. If your passport is not a British one, you must ensure that you can gain re-entry into the UK.

HEALTH

Consider the temperature charts in your brochure - you probably want to feel comfortable, not too hot or too cold. Be aware of differing standards of hygiene and the prevalence of disease if your party includes children and older people. Your local health centre can advise on recommended vaccinations, inoculations and other precautions.

TYPES OF ACCOMMODATION

The choice is endless:

    Campsites
    Youth Hostels
    Bed and Breakfast
    Guest Houses and Pensions
    Houseboats and Yachts
    Small and large Hotels

Cost is probably the most important factor in choosing accommodation but consider the amount of work which may be involved in self-catering. Eating out varies enormously in price between resorts and countries - obtain a rough idea before you make your final decision.

On any holiday, there may be extra costs for which you had not planned - such as use of sun beds, sports facilities, local travel, extra films for your camera, etc.

FLIGHTS

The flight time may vary between 2 hours and 14 hours. Long distance flights sometimes include a re-fuelling stop. Some airlines are reluctant to allow women who are more than 28 weeks pregnant to fly without a doctor's letter. Check with your agent and your doctor.

When packing, remember that there is a maximum baggage allowance, and only one small piece of hand luggage is permitted.

1

Unit 4 Task 1 (cont.)

A copy of this letter has been forwarded to your travel agent, Rochley Travel, and I hope that you will visit them at your earliest opportunity to book your holiday of a lifetime and take advantage of our superb savings.

Yours sincerely
DISTANT LANDS PLC

Alison Louis

Enc

Copy to Rochley Travel

2

Unit 4 Task 3

INDIAN HOLIDAYS

GUIDELINES FOR INDIA

Choosing your perfect Indian holiday is part of the pleasure of the whole experience. However, you should choose with care to ensure full enjoyment.

MAKING AN INFORMED CHOICE

Read the details in the brochure carefully. The information will be accurate but, for example, you cannot afford to miss the fact that a hotel's access to the beach is by steep steps if you have infants or disabled persons in your party. Ask your agent for further details of your choice before booking.

On any Indian holiday, there may be extra costs for which you had not planned - such as use of sun beds, sports facilities, local travel, extra films for your camera, etc.

3

Unit 4 Task 2 (cont.)

FURTHER ASSISTANCE

These are general guidelines only. Your travel agent will be able to give detailed information and help. Read the small print in the holiday brochure too - you may not be aware of all the implications unless you do.

2

Unit 4 Task 3 (cont.)

INDIAN HOLIDAYS

MONEY

No Indian currency (rupees) may be imported or exported. You will have to complete a Declaration Form on arrival to state the amount of cash, notes and travellers' cheques you have brought. There is no limit to the amount. It is very important that you change money only through authorised money changers.

WHEN IN INDIA ...

Footwear should not be worn in Muslim, Hindu, Jain or Sikh temples. You should cover your head before going into a Sikh shrine.

It is best not to give money to beggars, and you should be careful not to succumb to 'bargains' from street vendors - use only government emporia and shops on the list published by the Department of Tourism.

5

Unit 4 Task 3 (cont.)

INDIAN HOLIDAYS

TYPES OF ACCOMMODATION

The choice is endless:

1   Campsites
2   Bed and Breakfast
3   Youth Hostels
4   Guest Houses and Pensions
5   Houseboats and Yachts
6   Small and large Hotels

Cost is probably the most important factor in choosing accommodation. Obtain a rough idea before you make your final decision.

On any Indian holiday, there may be extra costs for which you had not planned - such as use of sun beds, sports facilities, local travel, extra films for your camera, etc.

FLIGHTS

The flight time may vary between 8 hours and 14 hours, and sometimes include a re-fuelling stop. Some airlines are reluctant to allow women who are more than 28 weeks pregnant to fly without a doctor's letter. Check with your agent <u>and</u> your doctor.

When packing, remember that there is a maximum baggage allowance, and only one small piece of hand luggage is permitted.

4

Exercise 5B

MICROWAVE COOKING

VEGETABLE	COOK[1]	PROPORTIONS		MINS	SERVING SUGGESTIONS
		SIZE	WEIGHT		
Artichokes	T	Small	200 g (8 oz)	8	Butter & lemon juice
Artichokes	T or S	Pieces	25 g (1 oz)	4	Melted butter or white sauce
Cabbage	S	Shredded	n/a	4	Melted butter
Cauliflower	T or S	Florets	n/a	4	Cheese sauce
Courgettes	S	Whole[2]	50 g (2 oz)	3	Melted butter
Spinach	WT	Leaves	n/a	1	Melted butter

1 S = Separator, T = Trivet, WT = Without Trivet
2 If using 1-inch slices, increase cooking time to 4 minutes.

Exercise 5C

REF NO	PAGE	ITEM DESCRIPTION	SIZE	COST PER ITEM[1]	
				UNDER 10	OVER 10
26C	4	Fenn Sweatshirt	40-42	£18.99	£16.99
49D	5	Layton Sweatshirt[2]	36-38	£17.99	£15.99
18B	6	Mayling Sweatshirt	34-36	£16.99	£14.99
43Z	9	Harvest Sweatshirt	34-36	£16.99	£14.99

1 Orders of over 50 qualify for a further discount.
2 Limited stock available on this item.

Unit 4 Task 3 (cont.)

INDIAN HOLIDAYS

PASSPORTS AND VISAS

Allow yourself sufficient time to obtain a full passport and a visa. Check with your travel agent and the High Commission of India. If your passport is not a British one, you must ensure that you can gain re-entry into the UK.

HEALTH

Consider the temperature charts in your brochure - you probably want to feel comfortable, not too hot or too cold. Be aware of differing standards of hygiene and the prevalence of disease if your party includes children and older people.

A course of anti-malaria pills is recommended, and you should be inoculated against Cholera. It is generally a good idea to buy bottled mineral water. Don't forget to take with you any special medicines you are likely to need.

FURTHER ASSISTANCE

These are general guidelines only. Your travel agent will be able to give detailed information and help. Read the small print in the Indian holiday brochure too - you may not be aware of all the implications unless you do.

6

Exercise 6B

TELEPHONE MESSAGE FORM

Message for ....

Date .... Time ....

Caller's name ....

Caller's company ....

Caller's telephone number ....

Message ....

....

....

....

ACTION:

Urgent
Will call again later
Please ring back
Message left
(tick as appropriate)

Message taken by .... Ext no ....

Note: Your form layout may differ slightly from the print-out check above, but make sure that you have included the same information and that you have left sufficient space to the left of the ACTION list.

Exercise 5D

DESKTOP PCs

MACHINE	PRICE £	SPECIFICATION DETAILS			HARD DISK	M S D[2]
		PROCESSOR	SPEED	MEMORY[1]		
A) DIGIT-EX SYSTEMS						
Digit-ex Classic	825.00	i486SX	33MHz	4Mb-64Mb	210Mb	5
Digit-ex Royale	1459.00	i486DX	33MHz	4Mb-128Mb	250Mb	6
Digit-ex Magna	2774.00	Pentium	66MHz	16Mb-192Mb	520Mb	7
B) COMPUSTYLE TECHNO SYSTEMS						
CTS basic	599.00	Cx486SLC	33MHz	2Mb-16Mb	100Mb	4
CTS exec	1569.00	Am486DX	40MHz	4Mb-64Mb	260Mb	4
CTS de-luxe	1885.00	i486DX2	33MHz	8Mb-64Mb	340Mb	5
C) JRM DESKPRO SYSTEMS						
Value-line ZX2	899.00	i486SX	33MHz	4Mb-32Mb	200Mb	3
ZX3 Plus	1300.00	i486DX	33MHz	4Mb-64Mb	250Mb	5
ZX4 Super	1845.00	Pentium	66MHz	8Mb-64Mb	270Mb	5

[1] Standard and maximum on board.
[2] Maximum Storage Devices.

Exercise 6G

```
                                        J G GREENWOOD & SONS LTD
                                                 36 Hewitt Road
                                                      Sheffield
                                                       Grimsby
                                                       GR3 7UR

CUSTOMER NAME: Mrs Dawson

ADDRESS: 56 Ryder Crescent, Grimsby

TEL NO: Grimsby 583356

JOB REF NO: 672

JOB DESCRIPTION: Repairs to porch

JOB COMPLETED BY: Jim Watmough

PRICE: £370                         JOB COMPLETION DATE: 2 March 1995

PAYMENT METHOD: Cheque              PAYMENT DATE: 2 March 1995
```

Exercise 6D

BAYSWORTH SERVICES LTD
Staff Personnel Details

SURNAME: *

FIRST NAME: *

ADDRESS: *

Employment Basis:

full time
part time
temporary
permanent
probationary
casual
(please tick as appropriate)

TELEPHONE NUMBER: *

DATE OF BIRTH: *

N.I. NO: *

EMPLOYEE NO: *

JOB TITLE: *

DEPARTMENT: *

START DATE: *

Note: Your form layout may differ slightly from the print-out check above, but make sure that you have included the same information and that you have left sufficient space to the left of the Employment Basis list.

Exercise 6I

BAYSWORTH SERVICES LTD
Staff Personnel Details

SURNAME: Littlewood

FIRST NAME: Vanessa

ADDRESS: 32, Hardy Avenue. Harrogate, HG4 6TE

Employment Basis:

full time
part time ✓
temporary
permanent
probationary
casual ✓
(please tick as appropriate)

TELEPHONE NUMBER: Harrogate 652347

DATE OF BIRTH: 3 March 1959

N.I. NO: MB/42/73/A

EMPLOYEE NO: 698

JOB TITLE: Clerk

DEPARTMENT: Sales

START DATE: 31 March 1995   STARTING SALARY: £3.25 per hour

Exercise 6H

BAYSWORTH SERVICES LTD
Staff Personnel Details

SURNAME: McNamara

FIRST NAME: Julie

ADDRESS: 27 Greenbury Road, Leeds, LS3 4DB

Employment Basis:

full time ✓
part time
temporary
permanent
probationary ✓
casual
(please tick as appropriate)

TELEPHONE NUMBER: 0532 472234

DATE OF BIRTH: 26 August 1964

N.I. NO: YZ/12/89/46/A

EMPLOYEE NO: 697

JOB TITLE: Administrative Assistant

DEPARTMENT: Finance

START DATE: 12 April 1995   STARTING SALARY: £9,500 per annum

Exercise 7C

WALTON MANUFACTURING CO LTD

A meeting of the Walton Manufacturing Co Ltd will be held on *(date inserted for 15th of next month)* in the Board Room, Tunstall House, Chatsworth Lane, Chesterfield at 2.00pm.

A G E N D A

1   Apologies for absence

2   Minutes of last meeting

3   Matters arising from minutes

4   Financial Report

5   Recruitment review

6   Review of salary scales

7   Marketing strategy

8   Any other business

9   Date and time of next meeting

I J WELBECK
Honorary Secretary

Exercise 7A

HAMLET ROAD YOUTH CLUB

The Annual General Meeting of the Hamlet Road Youth Club will be held on *(date inserted for last Thursday of next month)* at the Club Centre at 1900 hours.

AGENDA

1   Apologies for absence

2   Minutes of last meeting

3   Matters arising from the minutes

4   Chairman's Annual Report

5   Treasurer's Annual Report

6   Programme plans for coming year

7   Any Other Business

N AKHTAR
Hon Secretary

Exercise 7F

Date of typing

Mrs P Agarwal
17 High Lane
Listerton
DENBRIDGE
DE10 2DI

Dear Mrs Agarwal

GRAND RE-OPENING

I have great pleasure in enclosing an invitation to the Exclusive Preview of our refurbished store.

You may have noticed that extensive alterations have been taking place recently and we would like you and your family as members to be among the first to enjoy a totally new shopping experience.

I look forward to welcoming you.

Yours sincerely

Marketing Manager

Enc

Letters also to: Mr W T Beechill and Dr M Ullah

Exercise 7E

Ref KL/CS/CPL1

Date of typing

Dear

Thank you for your communication of (date inserted for yesterday). I am sorry to hear that you have experienced a problem with the cooker which you purchased from

Your letter has been passed to us for attention.

In order to be able to deal with your complaint, we need the following information:

      Serial number
      Model number
      Date of purchase
      Nature of problem.

James Harvester will be dealing with the matter and I can assure you that your complaint will be carefully investigated. He will telephone you in the immediate future to obtain the necessary information.

I would like to thank you for drawing our attention to this matter. It is our company policy to encourage customer feedback and we welcome the opportunity to improve our product and our service.

Yours sincerely
RADFORD & MUSKHAM LTD

KATHERINE LEHRER
Customer Services Manager

Exercise 7G (cont.)

Date of typing

Mr W T Beechill
Clevely House
Roundhill
LUNDLEY
LY3 3RJ

Dear Mr Beechill

GRAND RE-OPENING

I have great pleasure in enclosing an invitation to the Exclusive Preview of our refurbished store.

You may have noticed that extensive alterations have been taking place recently and we would like you and your family as VIP members to be among the first to enjoy a totally new shopping experience.

I look forward to welcoming you.

Yours sincerely

Marketing Manager

Enc

Letters also to: Mrs P Agarwal and Mrs K Clare

Exercise 7F (cont.)

Title	FirstName	LastName	Address1	Address2	City	PostalCode	Membership
Mrs	P	Agarwal	17 High Lane	Listerton	DENBRIDGE	DE10 2DI	VIP
Dr	M	Ullah	Moorside	Rapley Green	ANWORTH	AH11 2HM	Star
Mr	W T	Beechill	Clevely House	Roundhill	LUNDLEY	LY3 3RJ	VIP

Exercise 7G

Title	FirstName	LastName	Address1	Address2	City	PostalCode	Membership
Mrs	P	Agarwal	17 High Lane	Listerton	DENBRIDGE	DE10 2DI	VIP
Dr	M	Ullah	Moorside	Rapley Green	ANWORTH	AH11 2HM	Star
Mr	W T	Beechill	Clevely House	Roundhill	LUNDLEY	LY3 3RJ	VIP
Miss	G M	O'Dowd	146 Willow Crescent	Langford	JAMESTOWN	JN7 8AL	Star
Mrs	K	Clare	25 Second Avenue	Crofton	NUTFIELD	ND4 3DN	VIP

Exercise 7H

Title	FirstName	LastName	Address1	Address2	City	PostalCode	Retailer
Mr and Mrs	R P	Jarvis	Churchfield	21 Church Lane	HOL MEV ILLE	HE1 7RL	Gregson & Waite Ltd
Mr	B	Surley	27 Orchard Way	Hammerfield	LON GLA ND	LD8 8DH	Gregson & Waite Ltd
Miss	Shazia	Hasan	37 Grange Court	Worthwood	NOR TON BUR Y	NY5 4ZX	Euro Electrics PLC
Mr	T	Knapp	Eastfield Manor	Eastfield	WHE RTO N	WN11 7NR	Euro Electrics PLC
Mrs	Pauline	Moran	10 Emsley Park Drive	Emsley	NOR TON BUR Y	NY3 6MJ	Euro Electrics PLC
Ms	Susannah	Bruno	Dean Hill	Vernon Road	WHE RTO N	WN9 3JS	Gregson & Waite Ltd
Mr and Mrs	J F	Spencer	12 Windsor Grove	Hammerfield	LON GLA ND	LD8 7SU	Gregson & Waite Ltd
Mr	I J	Royd	16 James Street	Vale Moor	LOW CRO FT	LT6 9FC	Euro Electrics PLC
Mrs	L A	Wachewska	Oak House	Mount	ALL ANT ON	AN8 6PJ	Gregson & Waite Ltd
Mr	Thomas	Van-Helf	10 Dodgson Avenue	Dene Green	CAM TON	CN4 3MA	Gregson & Waite Ltd

Exercise 7H (cont.)

Ref KL/CS/CPL1

Date of typing

«Title» «FirstName» «LastName»
«Address1»
«Address2»
«City»
«PostalCode»

Dear «Title» «LastName»

Thank you for your communication of *(date inserted for yesterday)*. I am sorry to hear that you have experienced a problem with the cooker which you purchased from «Retailer».

Your letter has been passed to us for attention.

In order to be able to deal with your complaint, we need the following information:

    Serial number
    Model number
    Date of purchase
    Nature of problem.

James Harvester will be dealing with the matter and I can assure you that your complaint will be carefully investigated. He will telephone you in the immediate future to obtain the necessary information.

I would like to thank you for drawing our attention to this matter. It is our company policy to encourage customer feedback and we welcome the opportunity to improve our product and our service.

Yours sincerely
RADFORD & MUSKHAM LTD

KATHERINE LEHRER
Customer Services Manager

Exercise 8A – Part 1

FERNDALE THEATRE BOOKING FORM

Name: _____

Address: _____ Postcode: _____

Telephone: day: _____ evening: _____

I wish to make the following booking:

Production: _____ Date: _____ Venue: _____

No of tickets: _____

Ticket price: _____

Payment Method (please tick as appropriate):

☐ A) I authorise you to debit my Access/Visa account number *(delete as appropriate)*:

_____

Expiry date: _____ Signed: _____

☐ B) I enclose a Cheque/Postal Order for the total amount made payable to Ferndale Council.

Please complete and return with payment to:

Ferndale Theatre Box Office
27-29 Reighton Road
FERNDALE
FD7 4AG

Note: Your layout may not be identical to the example given here, but you should have included all the relevant information shown.

Exercise 7H (cont.)

Ref KL/CS/CPL1

Date of typing

Mr and Mrs R P Jarvis
Churchfield
21 Church Lane
HOLMEVILLE
HE1 7RL

Dear Mr and Mrs Jarvis

Thank you for your communication of *(date inserted for yesterday)*. I am sorry to hear that you have experienced a problem with the cooker which you purchased from Gregson & Waite Ltd.

Your letter has been passed to us for attention.

In order to be able to deal with your complaint, we need the following information:

      Serial number
      Model number
      Date of purchase
      Nature of problem.

James Harvester will be dealing with the matter and I can assure you that your complaint will be carefully investigated. He will telephone you in the immediate future to obtain the necessary information.

I would like to thank you for drawing our attention to this matter. It is our company policy to encourage customer feedback and we welcome the opportunity to improve our product and our service.

Yours sincerely
RADFORD & MUSKHAM LTD

KATHERINE LEHRER
Customer Services Manager

Letters also to: Mr B Surley, Ms Susannah Bruno, Mr and Mrs J F Spencer, Mrs L A Wachewska and Mr Thomas Van-Helf

Exercise 8A – Part 2

FERNDALE THEATRE BOOKING FORM

Name: @

Address: @

Postcode: @

Telephone: day: @   evening: @

Method of payment: @

If paying by Visa or Access: Credit card number: @

Expiry date of credit card: @

Customer signature obtained *(enter YES or NO)*: @

Production: @

Venue: @

Date: @

No of tickets: @

Ticket price: @

Total payment: @

Exercise 8B

FERNDALE THEATRE MONTHLY PLANNER

The events tabled below are proposed for October and November, and are scheduled to be held in one of the Ferndale Theatre venues shown below:

Venue A - St Mary's Hall
Venue B - The Grande
Venue C - Pickwick Studios.

START DATE	PRODUCTION	COMPANY NAME/ ARTIST	TICKET PRICES (£) A^1	B^2	C^3	VENUE
OCTOBER						
02/10/95	Macbeth	Lowe Theatre Company	21.00	17.00	------	A
09/10/95	Coppelia	Ryedale Theatre Ballet	19.50	15.50	------	B
11/10/95	Oliver to Music	GRS Operatic Society	18.50	13.00	10.00	A
16/10/95	Strauss Night	The Robem Orchestra	14.00	11.00	------	B
23/10/95	Pinnochio	Saldale Puppet Company	11.50	8.50	5.00	C
NOVEMBER						
02/11/95	Lord of the Rings	Barton Theatrical	19.50	15.50	13.50	B
10/11/95	PlayAway Days	Kiddishows Inc.	10.00	7.00	4.50	C
16/11/95	Tropical Nights	Peacock Dance Theatre	16.00	13.00	------	A
18/11/95	Variety Showbar	Ferndale Music Society	14.50	11.50	------	B
26/11/95	Ray Varnour	Ray Varnour & Showband	21.00	17.00	9.50	B

[1] Friday and Saturday evenings - 20% discounts for Children, Students, Over 60s.
[2] Tuesday to Thursday evenings - 30% discounts for Children, Students, Over 60s.
[3] Matinees only - no discounts available.

Exercise 8C

Title	FirstName	LastName	Address1	Address2	City	PostalCode	membership
Ms	Rachel	Coombes	24 Barber Grove	Leighton	CRAGLAND	CD5 6PJ	Ordinary
Mr & Mrs	C	Janes	Kingston House	Stoneley	STONEFORD	SD11 6JM	Concessionary
Ms	Louisa	Deneve	146 Long Road	Burkiston	BELLWOOD	BW7 3MO	Ordinary
Mrs	G	Dziaszyk	Easter Cottage	Easter Lane	CRAGLAND	CD4 3NT	Ordinary
Mr	T	Heine	6 Feitham Grove	Burkiston	BELLWOOD	BW3 6MJ	Concessionary
Miss	Rebecca	Martyn	160 Westland Avenue	Top Scarr	SCAR HILL	SC22 4FG	Concessionary
Rev	P W	Wright	The Vicarage	Oakley	STONEFORD	SD7 8VG	Ordinary
Dr	Peter	Anstruther	Margaret's House	Lady Road	ROYDLEY	RO8 4PB	Concessionary
Mr & Mrs	Johann	Pesendorfer	16 Lake View Terrace	Lakeside	LOUGHTON	LN8 6PW	Concessionary
Miss	Esther	Beckett	1 May Green	Top Scarr	SCAR HILL	SC20 6LH	Concessionary

Exercise 8C (cont.)

Ref FT/MS/AS070

Date of typing

«Title» «FirstName» «LastName»
«Address1»
«Address2»
«City»
«PostalCode»

Dear «Title» «LastName»

AUTUMN SEASON

Our new Autumn programme offers something for everyone from Shakespeare and Strauss to Pinnochio and Vaudeville. There's a special fun-packed show for the children where audience participation is not just encouraged, it is expected!

As a «membership» subscription member, you can take advantage of reduced prices and priority booking. Our monthly planner and booking form are enclosed, together with the Autumn programme brochure.

Enjoy browsing through the brochure but don't take too long! Return your booking form as soon as possible to ensure the dates and seats you require.

Happy theatre-going!

Yours sincerely

Judith O'Conner
BOX OFFICE MANAGER

Encs

Exercise 8C (cont.)

Ref FT/MS/AS070

Date of typing

Mr & Mrs C Janes
Kingston House
Stoneley
STONEFORD
SD11 6JM

Dear Mr & Mrs Janes

AUTUMN SEASON

Our new Autumn programme offers something for everyone from Shakespeare and Strauss to Pinnochio and Vaudeville. There's a special fun-packed show for the children where audience participation is not just encouraged, it is expected!

As a Concessionary subscription member, you can take advantage of reduced prices and priority booking. Our monthly planner and booking form are enclosed, together with the Autumn programme brochure.

Enjoy browsing through the brochure but don't take too long! Return your booking form as soon as possible to ensure the dates and seats you require.

Happy theatre-going!

Yours sincerely

Judith O'Conner
BOX OFFICE MANAGER

Encs

Letters also to: Mr T Heine, Miss Rebecca Martyn, Dr Peter Anstruther, Mr & Mrs Johann Pesendorfer, Miss Esther Beckett

Progress review checklist

Unit	Topic	Date completed	Comments
1	Apostrophe exercises		
	Exercise 1A Letter on letterhead		
	Exercise 1B Letter on letterhead		
	Exercise 1C Letter with continuation sheet		
2	Exercise 2A Two-page document		
	Exercise 2A Applied Character Style		
	Exercise 2B Modified Character Style		
3	AutoCorrect exercise		
	Exercise 3A Amended multi-page document		
	Exercise 3B Amended multi-page document		
4	Consolidation 1		
5	Footnotes exercises		
	Table practice exercises		
	Exercise 5B Table		
	Exercise 5C Table		
	Exercise 5D Table		
6	Exercise 6A Borders and shading practice exercises		
	Exercise 6B Telephone message form		
	Exercise 6C Form with entry points		
	Exercise 6D Personnel form		
	Exercise 6E Drawing practice		
	Exercise 6F Form using drawing tools		
	Exercise 6G Form completion		
	Exercise 6H Form completion		
	Exercise 6I Form completion		
	Exercise 6J Word's form fields exercise		
7	Exercise 7C Notice and Agenda from stored standard files		
	Exercise 7D AutoText creation		
	Exercise 7E Letter from stored AutoText		
	Exercise 7F Mail Merge exercises		
	Exercise 7G Mail Merge selected records		
	Exercise 7H Mail Merge selected records		
8	Consolidation 2		

Glossary

Action ☞	Keyboard ⌨	Mouse 🖱	Menu 📄
Allocate clear lines	Press: ↵ once for each line required, plus one		
Allocate vertical space			Format, Paragraphs Key in measurement
AutoCorrect			Tools, AutoCorrect
AutoText Create an AutoText entry	n/a	Key in and select text to be stored Click: 🔲 on Standard Tool Bar Name the entry. Click: Add	Key in and select text to be stored Select: Edit, AutoText Name the entry. Click: Add
Insert an AutoText entry	Position insertion point Type: Name of AutoText entry Press: F3	Position insertion point Type: Name of AutoText entry Click: 🔲 on Standard Tool Bar	Position insertion point Select: Edit, AutoText Click: Insert button
Blocked capitals	Press: Caps lock key		
Boilerplating	See AutoText or Standard paragraph files		
Borders and shading		Click: ▦ on Formatting Tool Bar Select: appropriate option(s) from the Borders Tool Bar	Format, Borders and Shading Select: Borders or Shading Select a line style or shading percentage Click: OK
Bold text	Press: Ctrl + B	Click: 🔲 on Formatting Tool Bar	Format, Font
Bulleted lists		Click: 🔲 on Formatting Tool Bar	Format, Bullets and Numbering
Case of letters	Press: Shift + F3 To capitalize letters: Press: Ctrl + Shift + A		Format, Change case
Centre text	Press: Ctrl + E	Click: 🔲 on Formatting Tool Bar	Format, Paragraphs, Indents and Spacing, Alignment
Close a file (clear screen)	Press: Ctrl + C		File, Close
Copy a block of text Select text to be copied	Press: Ctrl + C	Click: 🔲 on Standard Tool Bar or Press: Right mouse button and Select: Copy	Edit, Copy
Position cursor where text is to be copied to	Press: Ctrl + V	Click: 🔲 on Standard Tool Bar or Press: Right mouse button and select: Paste	Edit, Paste
Cursor movement Move cursor to required position	Use arrow keys ↑ ↓ ← →	Click: Left mouse button in required position	
Move to top of document	Ctrl + Home		
Move to end of document	Ctrl + End		
Move left word by word	Ctrl + ←		
Move right word by word	Ctrl + →		
Move to end of line	End		
Move to start of line	Home		
Cut text	See Delete/cut a block of text		
Date insertion	Press: Alt + Shift + D		Insert, Date and Time
Delete a character	Move cursor to incorrect character: Press: Del or Move cursor to right of incorrect character: Press ← (Del)		
Delete a word	Move cursor to end of word: Press: Ctrl + ← (Del) or Ctrl + X	Double-click on word to select: Press: Right mouse button Select: Cut	Select incorrect word: Select: Edit, Cut
Delete/cut a block of text	Select incorrect text: Press: ← (Del) or select word: Press: Ctrl + X	Select incorrect text: Press: Right mouse button Select: Cut	Select incorrect text: Select: Edit, Cut
Drawing tools		Click: 🔲 on Standard Tool Bar Select: Appropriate drawing tool from the Drawing Tool Bar buttons	View, Toolbars, Click: the Drawing option 'on' Select: Appropriate drawing tool from the Drawing Tool Bar buttons
Entry points – to set up – to search for	Use a suitable symbol for the entry point which does not normally appear in the main text, e.g. $ or @ Operate Word's Find or Replace Command to locate the entry point, then replace with appropriate information		

Action ☞	Keyboard ⌨	Mouse ✋	Menu 📄
Exit the program	Press: **Alt + F4**	Double-click control button at left of title bar	<u>F</u>ile, E<u>x</u>it
Find text	Press: **Ctrl + F**		<u>E</u>dit, <u>F</u>ind
Font size	Press: **Ctrl + Shift + P** Choose desired size	Click: 🔟 ⬇ on Formatting Tool Bar Choose desired size	F<u>o</u>rmat, <u>F</u>ont Choose desired size
Next larger point size Next smaller point size	Press: **Ctrl +]** Press: **Ctrl + [**		
Font typeface style	Press: **Ctrl + Shift + F** Choose desired font	Click: Times New Roman ⬇ on Formatting Tool Bar Choose desired font	F<u>o</u>rmat, <u>F</u>ont Choose desired font
Footers			<u>V</u>iew, <u>H</u>eader and Footer Click: Switch between header and footer button. Key in footer text Click on **OK**
To delete a footer			<u>V</u>iew, <u>H</u>eader and Footer Select: Text in footer box and delete
Footnotes – using Word's automatic Footnote Command	Press: **Alt + Ctrl + F**		<u>I</u>nsert, Foot<u>n</u>ote, <u>F</u>ootnote, **AutoNumber** Select: <u>O</u>ptions to modify the footnote Click: **OK**
Footnotes – using superscript	Press: **Ctrl + Shift** + = to change font to superscript Key in the footnote character (number, letter or symbol) Press: **Ctrl + Shift** + = again to revert to normal text		
Foreign accents	è : **Ctrl + `** *(accent-grave)*, **the letter** é : **Ctrl + '** *(apostrophe)*, **the letter** ê : **Ctrl + ^** *(caret)*, **the letter** ä : **Ctrl + :** *(colon)*, **the letter** å : **Ctrl + @**, *a* or *A* õ : **Ctrl + ~** *(tilde)*, **the letter** æ : **Ctrl + &**, *a, o, A, O* ø : **Ctrl + /**, *o* or *O* ç : **Ctrl + ,** *(comma)*, *c* or *C* ð : **Ctrl + '** *(apostrophe)*, *d* or *D*		
Form Tool Bar			<u>F</u>ile, <u>N</u>ew Click on: Template button, OK Select: <u>T</u>oolbars from the <u>V</u>iew menu Click: the Forms option 'on'
Frame – to insert		Click: 🖼 on Drawing Tool Bar	<u>I</u>nsert, F<u>r</u>ame
Go to (a specified page)	Press: **Ctrl + G** *or* **F5**		<u>E</u>dit, <u>G</u>o To ...
Grammar tool			<u>T</u>ools, <u>G</u>rammar
Headers			<u>V</u>iew, <u>H</u>eader and Footer Key in header text. Click on OK
To delete a header			<u>V</u>iew, <u>H</u>eader and Footer Select: Text in header box and delete
Help function	Press: **F1** (for contents) Press: **Shift + F1** (for context sensitive help)	Click: ▶? on Formatting Tool Bar	<u>H</u>elp
Indent function Indent at left to next tab stop	Press: **Ctrl + M**	Click: ▤ on Formatting Tool Bar	F<u>o</u>rmat, <u>P</u>aragraphs, <u>I</u>ndents and Spacing
Indent at left to previous tab stop Indent as a hanging paragraph Unindent and return to standard margins	Press: **Ctrl + Shift + M** Press: **Ctrl + T** Press: **Ctrl + Q**	Click: ▤ on Formatting Tool Bar *using ruler:* First-line indent Left indent First-line and left indents Right indent	
Insert a line break	Press: **Shift + ↵**		
Insert a page break	Press: **Ctrl + ↵**		<u>I</u>nsert, <u>B</u>reak, Page break

Action ☞	Keyboard ⌨	Mouse 🖰	Menu 📄
Insert special characters/symbols	Press: **Ctrl + Shift + Q**		Position cursor where you want the character/symbol to appear: Select: **I**nsert, **S**ymbol
Insert text	Simply key in the missing character(s) at the appropriate place – the existing text will 'move over' to make room for the new text.		
Italics	Press: **Ctrl + I**	Click: *I* on Formatting Tool Bar	**F**ormat, **F**ont
Justified right margin	Press: **Ctrl + J**	Click: ▤ on Formatting Tool Bar	F**o**rmat, **P**aragraphs, **I**ndents and Spacing, Alignment
Line length – to change	Select text. Display horizontal ruler. Move margin markers to required position on ruler.		
Line spacing – to set	Press: **Ctrl + 1** (single) Press: **Ctrl + 2** (double) Press: **Ctrl + 0** (to add or delete a line space)		F**o**rmat, **P**aragraphs, **I**ndents and Spacing
Mailmerge – a) create main document	Key in the form letter and save the file using normal save procedures: Select: **T**ools, Mailme**r**ge, **C**reate, Form **L**etters Click: **A**ctive Window		
Mailmerge – b) create data source	After following mailmerge step a): Select: **G**et Data, **C**reate Data Source Add or remove field names as required Click: OK		
Mailmerge – c) save data source	After following mailmerge step b): With the Save Data Source dialogue box on screen: Key in appropriate name in File **N**ame box. Select: appropriate **D**irectory and Dri**v**e. Click: OK Select: Edit **D**ata Source – to go to Data Form and enter details fo reach record *or* Select: Edit **M**ain Document – to add merge fields to the Form Letter		
Mailmerge – d) edit data source (enter record details)	After following mailmerge step c) and selecting: Edit **D**ata Source Key in the information for each individual record – Click on: **A**dd New when each record is complete When all records are entered, Click: OK		
Mailmerge – e) print data source	Click: **E**dit data Source button on Mailmerge Tool Bar Click: **V**iew Source button in Data Form dialogue box Print in the normal way		
Mailmerge – f) insert merge codes in main document	With the Mailmerge Tool Bar on screen: Move insertion point to position of first merge code entry: Click: Insert Merge Field button on Mailmerge Tool Bar and select field name required from drop-down menu Repeat for each merge field code required		
Mailmerge – g) print the form letter	With the form letter displayed on screen, print in the normal way		
Mailmerge – h) view merged file	In the main document window: Click: View Merged Data button on Mailmerge Tool Bar (the first record appears) To view other records: Click on the arrow buttons on the Mailmerge Tool Bar *or* Key in the number of the required record between the arrows		
Mailmerge – i) print merged file	In the main document window: Click: Merge to Printer button on Mailmerge Tool Bar		
Mailmerge – j) merge specific records	Click: Mailmerge Helper button on Mailmerge Tool Bar Click: Query Options and select appropriate field in the Field box Select: Equal To from the Comparison drop-down menu Key in required criterion in the Compare To box. Click: OK. Close the Mailmerge Helper dialogue box View the merged file to check selection before printing. Save the merged file		
Margins (to change)			**F**ile, Page Set**u**p, **M**argins
Move a block of text Select text to be moved Position cursor where text is to be moved to	Press: **Ctrl + X** *or* **F2** Press: **Ctrl + V** *or* ↵ *or* Hold down **Ctrl** and Click: Right mouse button	Click: ✂ on Standard Tool Bar Click: 📋 on Standard Tool Bar *Drag and drop moving:* Select text to be moved Click left mouse button in middle of text and keep held down Drag selection to required location Release mouse button	**E**dit, Cu**t** **E**dit, **P**aste
Move around text quickly Left/right word by word End/start of line Top/bottom of paragraph Up/down one screen Top/bottom of document	Press: **Ctrl + ←** *or* **Ctrl + →** Press: **End** *or* **Home** Press: **Ctrl + ↑** *or* **Ctrl + ↓** Press: **PgUp** *or* **PgDn** Press: **Ctrl + Home** *or* **Ctrl + End**		
Open an existing file	Press: **Ctrl + O**	Click: 📂 on Standard Tool Bar	**F**ile, **O**pen
Open a new file	Press: **Ctrl + N**	Click: 📄 on Standard Tool Bar	**F**ile, **N**ew

Action ☞	Keyboard ⌨	Mouse 🖰	Menu 📄
Page numbering to delete page numbering	Press: Alt + Shift + P		**Insert, Page Numbers** **View, Header and Footer** Select the page numbers and delete
Page setup			**File, Page Setup** (Choose from **Margins, Paper Size,** **Paper Source** and **Layout**)
Paragraphs – splitting/joining	Make a new paragraph (i.e. split a paragraph into two) Join two consecutive paragraphs into one	Move cursor to first letter of new paragraph Press: ↵ twice Move cursor to first character of second paragraph Press: ← (**Del**) twice (backspace delete key) Press: **Spacebar** (to insert a space after full stop)	
Print out hard copy	Press: **Ctrl + P**	Click: 🖨 on Standard Tool Bar	**File, Print**
Ragged right margin	Press: **Ctrl + L**	Click: ▤ on Formatting Tool Bar	**Format, Paragraphs, Indents and** **Spacing, Alignment**
Remove text emphasis	Press: **Ctrl + Spacebar** *or* Press: **Ctrl + Shift + Z**	Select text to be changed back to normal text: Click: Appropriate button on Formatting Tool Bar	**Format, Paragraphs, Indents and** **Spacing**
Repeating actions	Press: **F4** to repeat previous action *or* Press: **Ctrl + Y**	Click: 🔁 on Formatting Tool Bar	To repeat sets of actions, drag down the **Redo** drop-down list and select the group of actions you wish to repeat

Replace text – typeover	1 Select the incorrect text and then type in the correct entry – Word will fit the replacement text exactly
	   into the original space
	2 Move cursor to incorrect entry:
	   Press: The **Ins** key (typeover on) and overtype with correct entry
	   Press: The **Ins** key again (typeover off) to stop overtyping text		

Restore deleted text	Press: **Ctrl + Z**	Click: 🔁 on Formatting Tool Bar	**Edit, Undo**
Ruler – to display			**View, Ruler**
Save work to disk Save a file for the first time Save an active file which has been saved previously Save *all* open files	Press: **F12** Press: **Ctrl + S** *or* Press: **Shift + F12**	Click: 💾 on Standard Toolbar Click: 💾 on Standard Tool Bar	**File, Save As** Enter **Filename** Select correct **Directory** and **Drive** Click on **OK** **File, Save** **File, Save All**
Scroll bars (to view)			**Tools, Options, View** Select: **Horizontal** scroll bar and **Vertical** scroll bar options
Search for text	*See* Find text.		
Select text One character (or more) One word To end of line Start of line A full line A paragraph Whole document Any block of text Remove selection	Press: **Shift** + ← *or* → Press: **Shift + Ctrl** + ← *or* → Press: **Shift + End** Press: **Shift + Home** Press: **Shift + End** *or* **Home** — Press: **Ctrl + A** —	Click and drag pointer across text Double-click on word Click and drag pointer right or down Click and drag pointer left or up Click in selection border Double-click in selection border Triple-click in selection border Position pointer at start of text and Press: **Shift**. Then, position pointer at end of text and click Click in any white space	
Sort (rearrange items)			Select the items or text to be sorted Select: **Table, Sort…**
Spaced capitals	Press: **Caps lock** key. Leave one space after each letter. Leave three spaces after each word.		
Spellcheck	Press: **F7**	Click: ✓ on Standard Tool Bar	**Tools, Spelling**
Standard paragraph files	*To store standard paragraphs:* Key in the portion of text to be saved as a standard paragraph file – save it in a separate file using normal *save* procedures *To insert standard paragraphs into your document:* Position insertion point where you want the standard paragraph to be inserted. Select: **File** from the **Insert** menu and select or key in the appropriate filename		

Action ☞	*Keyboard* ⌨	*Mouse* 🖰	*Menu* 📄
Status bar			Tools, Options, View Select: **Status Bar** option
Style – to create new			Format, **Style**, **New** Key in a style **Name** Select: Character from the style **Type** Select: **Font** from the Format menu Select: the text format from the options Click: OK, **Add** to Template, OK, Close
Style – to apply		Select: text to be formatted Select: required Style name from the Style drop-down menu on Formatting Tool Bar	Select: text to be formatted Format, **Style** Select: style required Click: **Apply**
Style – to modify			Format, **Style**, **Modify** Enter style name to be modified in the **Name** box Select: **Font** from the Format menu and make the required changes Click: OK, **Add** to Template, OK, Close
Superscript font	Press: **Ctrl + Shift + =**		Format, **Font**, **Superscript**
Switch on and load Word		Double-click **Microsoft Word** icon	
Symbols	*See* Insert special characters/symbols		
Table Wizard			Table, **Insert Table**, **Wizard**
Tables – to create (*see also* Unit 5)		Click: 🔲 on Standard Tool Bar	Table, **Insert Table**, **AutoFormat**
Tables with ruled lines	Pre-determine the borders and/or shading of the table layout using the Table Command or Table Wizard *or* Apply borders and/or shading after you have created the table display using the Borders and Shading command from the Format menu, or by using the Borders Tool Bar		
Tabulation Remove tabs	Select the paragraph(s) in which you wish to make changes to the tab settings, then either: 1 Select **Tabs** from the **Format** menu 2 Click the tab marker on the horizontal ruler line to select the type of tab you want, then drag the tab to the required position on the horizontal ruler line (*note:* Drag a tab marker *off* the horizontal ruler line to remove it)		
Text, replace	Press: **Ctrl + H**		Edit, **Replace**
Underline text Single word Double word	Press: **Ctrl + U** Press: **Ctrl + Shift + W** Press: **Ctrl + Shift + H**	Click: 🔲 on Formatting Tool Bar	Format, **Font**
Undoing actions	Press: **Ctrl + Z**	Click: 🔲 on Standard Tool Bar	To undo sets of actions, drag down the **Undo** drop-down list and select the group of actions you wish to undo
Units of measurement			Tools, **Options**, General **Measurement** Units Select desired units
View magnified pages		Click: 🔲 on Standard Tool Bar Click: **Magnifies** on print preview	View, **Zoom**
View – normal view	Press: **Ctrl + F2**	Click: 🔲 **Normal** button at bottom left of document window	View, **Normal**
View – outline view		Click: 🔲 **Outline** button at bottom left of document window	View, **Outline**
View – page layout view		Click: 🔲 **Page Layout** button at bottom left of document window	View, **Page Layout**
View – print preview	Press: **Ctrl + F2**	Click: 🔲 on Standard Tool Bar	File, **Print Preview**

Vertical column heading	Enter the heading one character per line so it is read downwards instead of across, e.g.: D
	       O
	       W
	       N		

Widow/orphan protection			Format, **Paragraph**, Text **Flow** Check that the ✕ is showing on the widow/orphan control box